Autumn And Thanksgiving Coloring Book For Kids

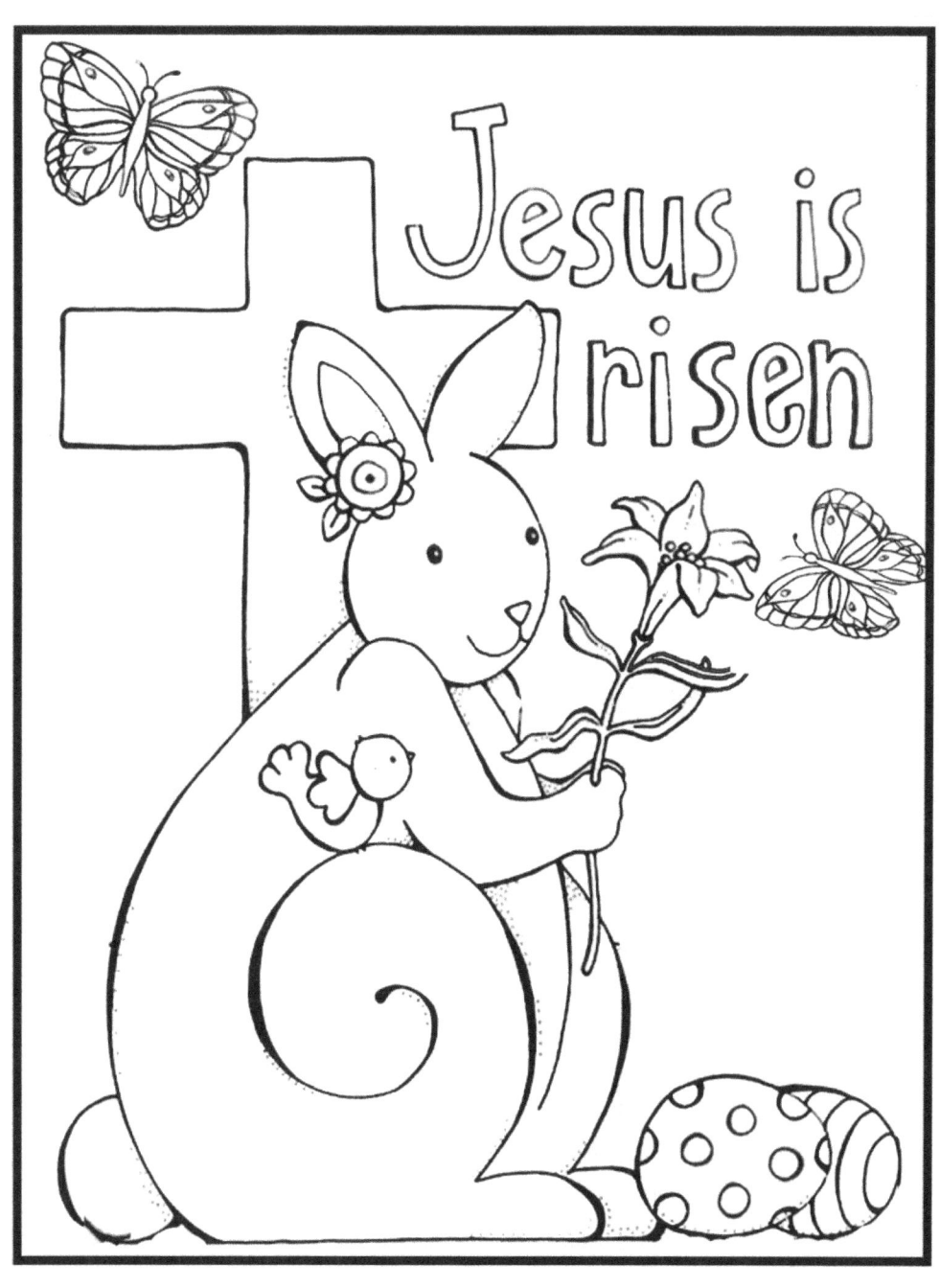

Nina.M

Autumn And Thanksgiving Coloring Book

A fun and festive Fall coloring adventure for children!

Copyright: Published in the United States by **Nina.M**
Published November 2017

All rights reserved. No part of this publication may be reproduced, stored in retrieval system, copied in any form or by any means, electronic, mechanical, photocopying, recording or otherwise transmitted without written permission from the publisher. Please do not participate in or encourage piracy of this material in any way. You must not circulate this book in any format Nina.M does not control or direct users' actions and is not responsible for the information or content shared, harm and/or actions of the book readers.

ISBN-13: 978-1979454438

ISBN-10: 1979454434

TODAY I'M THANKFUL FOR...

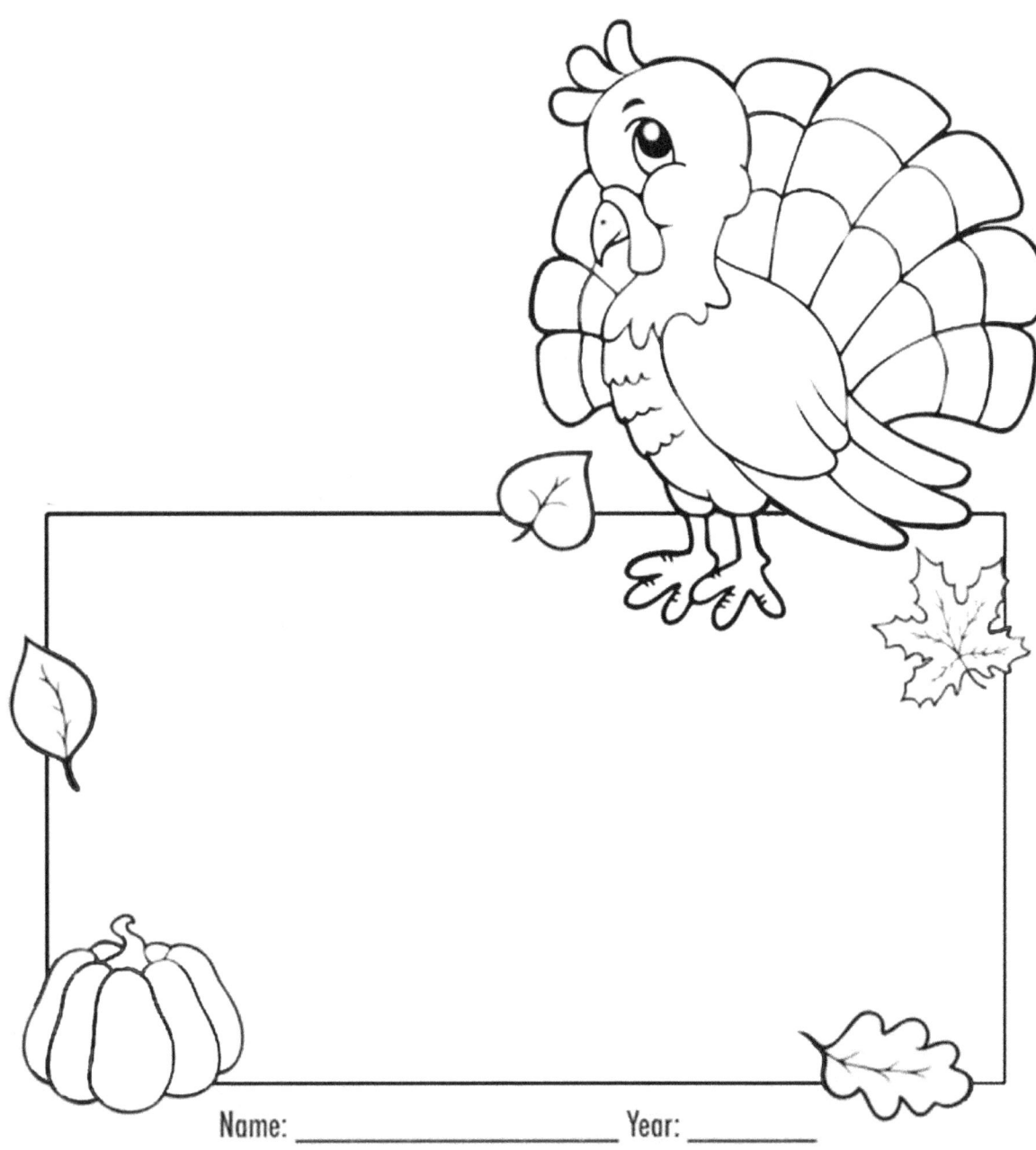

Name: _____ Year: _____

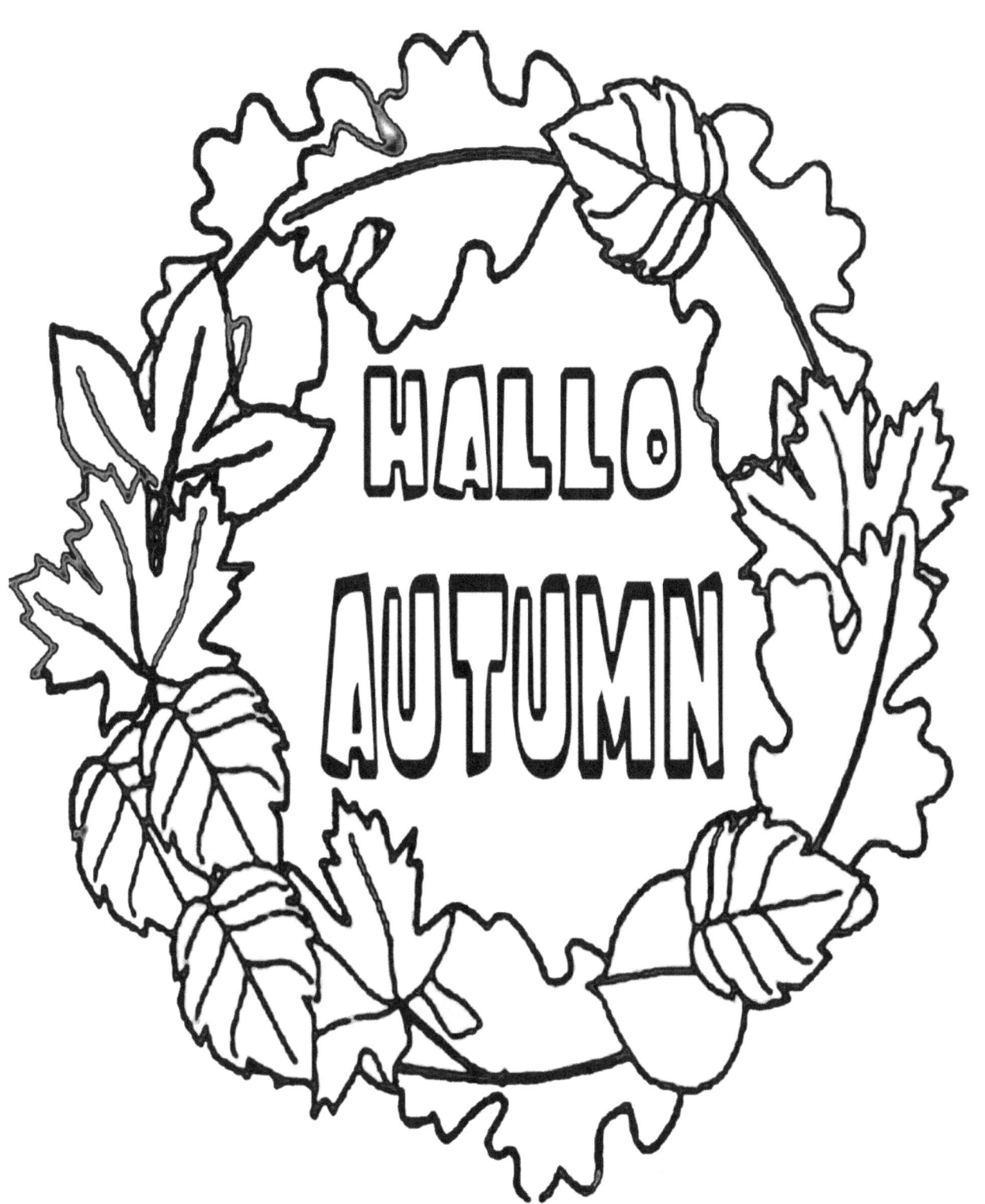

F is for Fall!

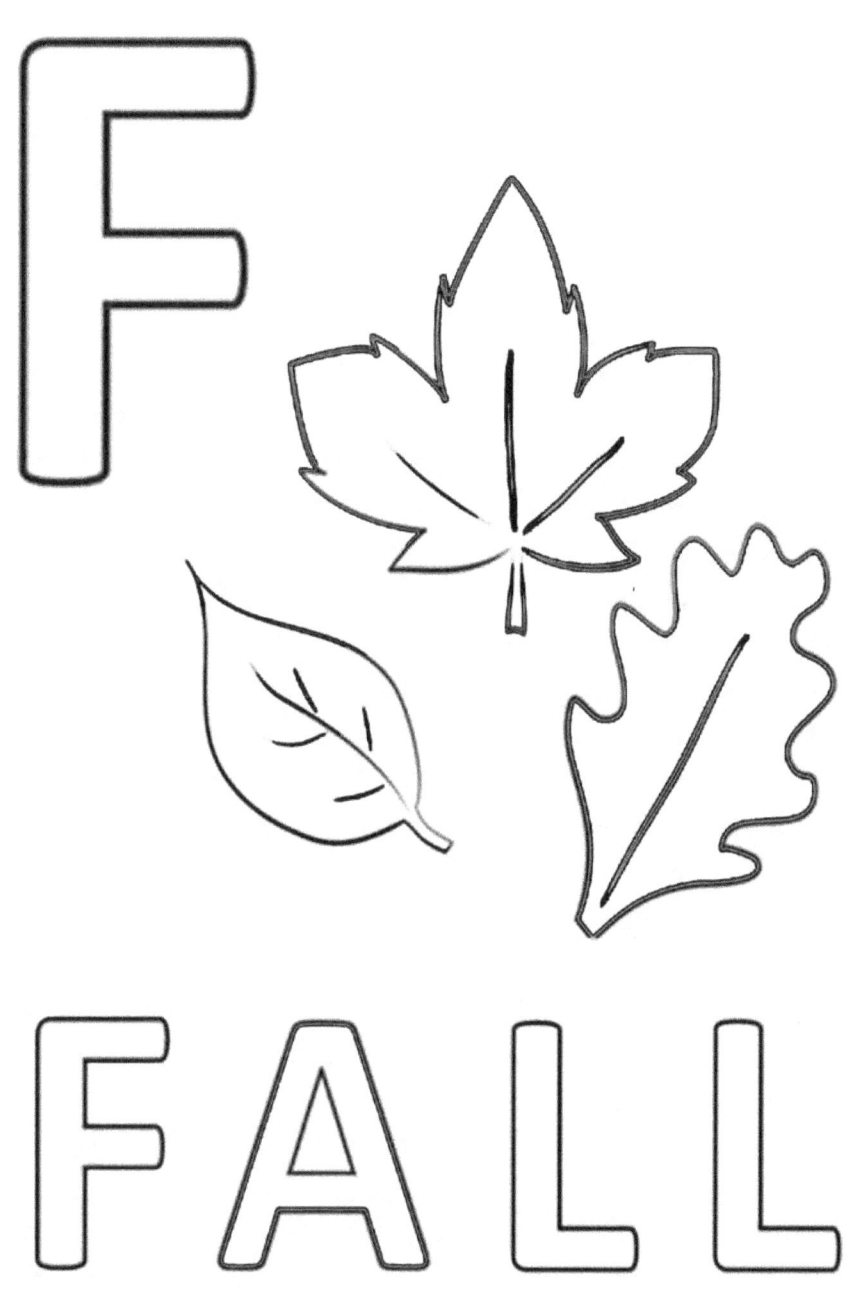

F

FALL

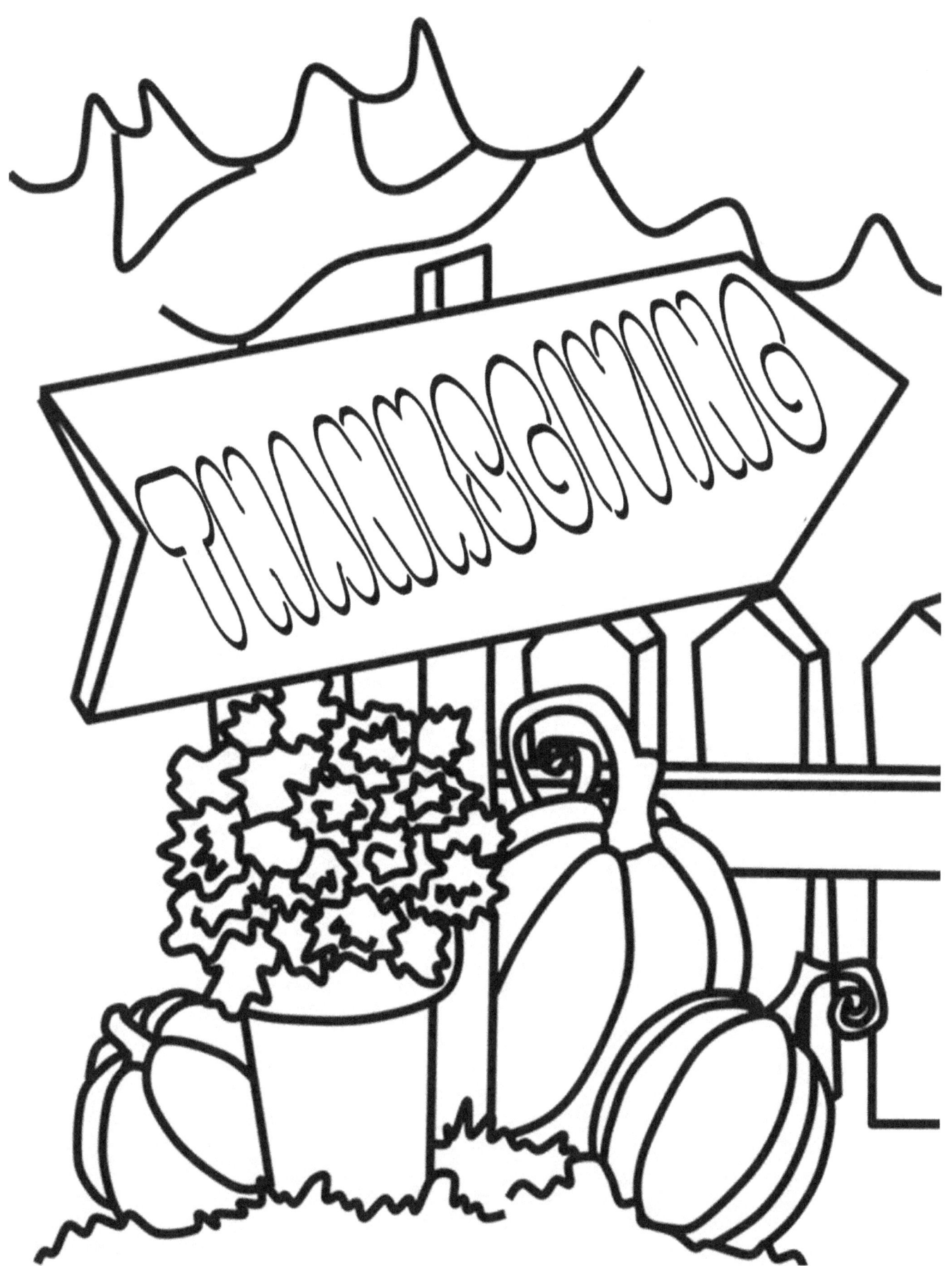

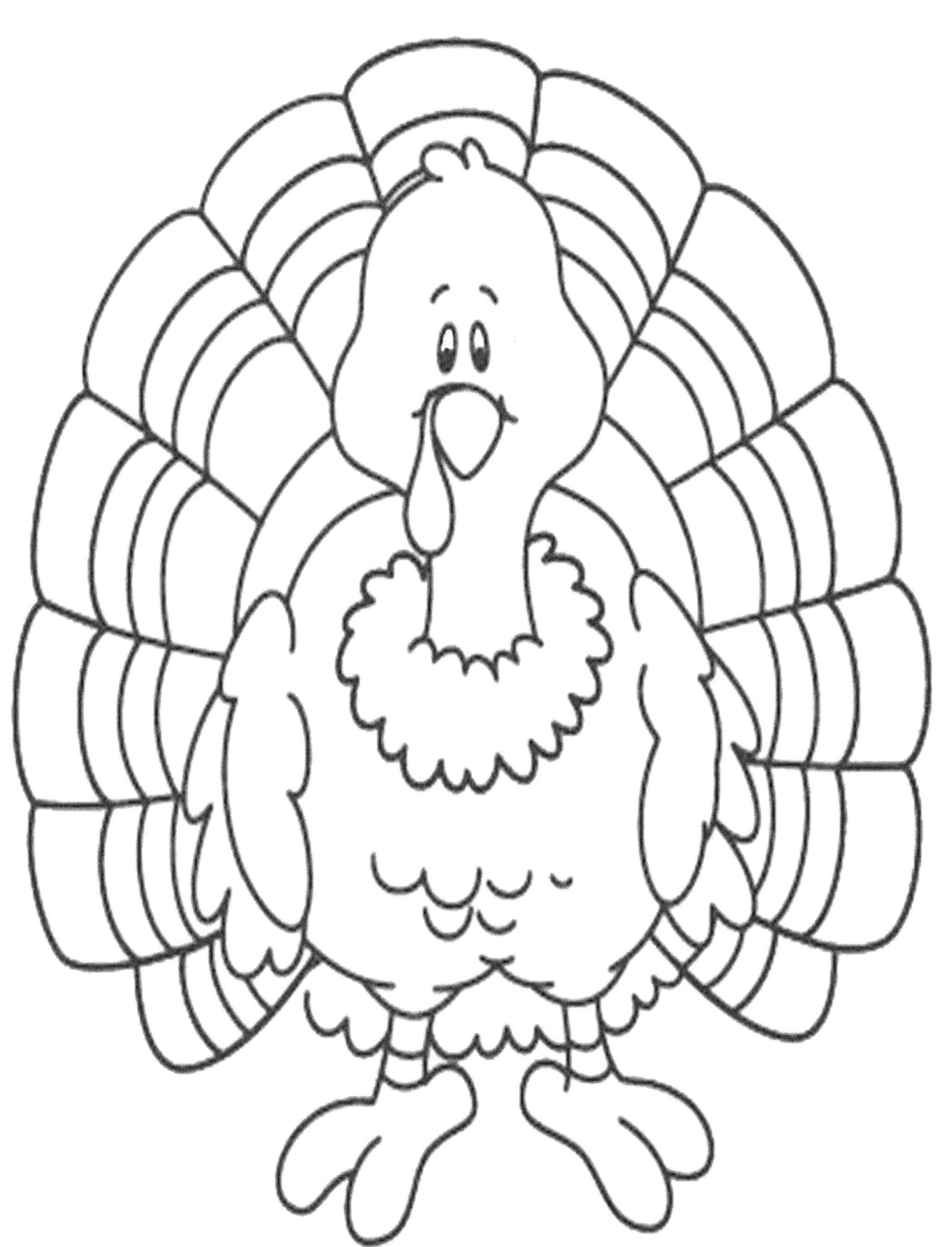

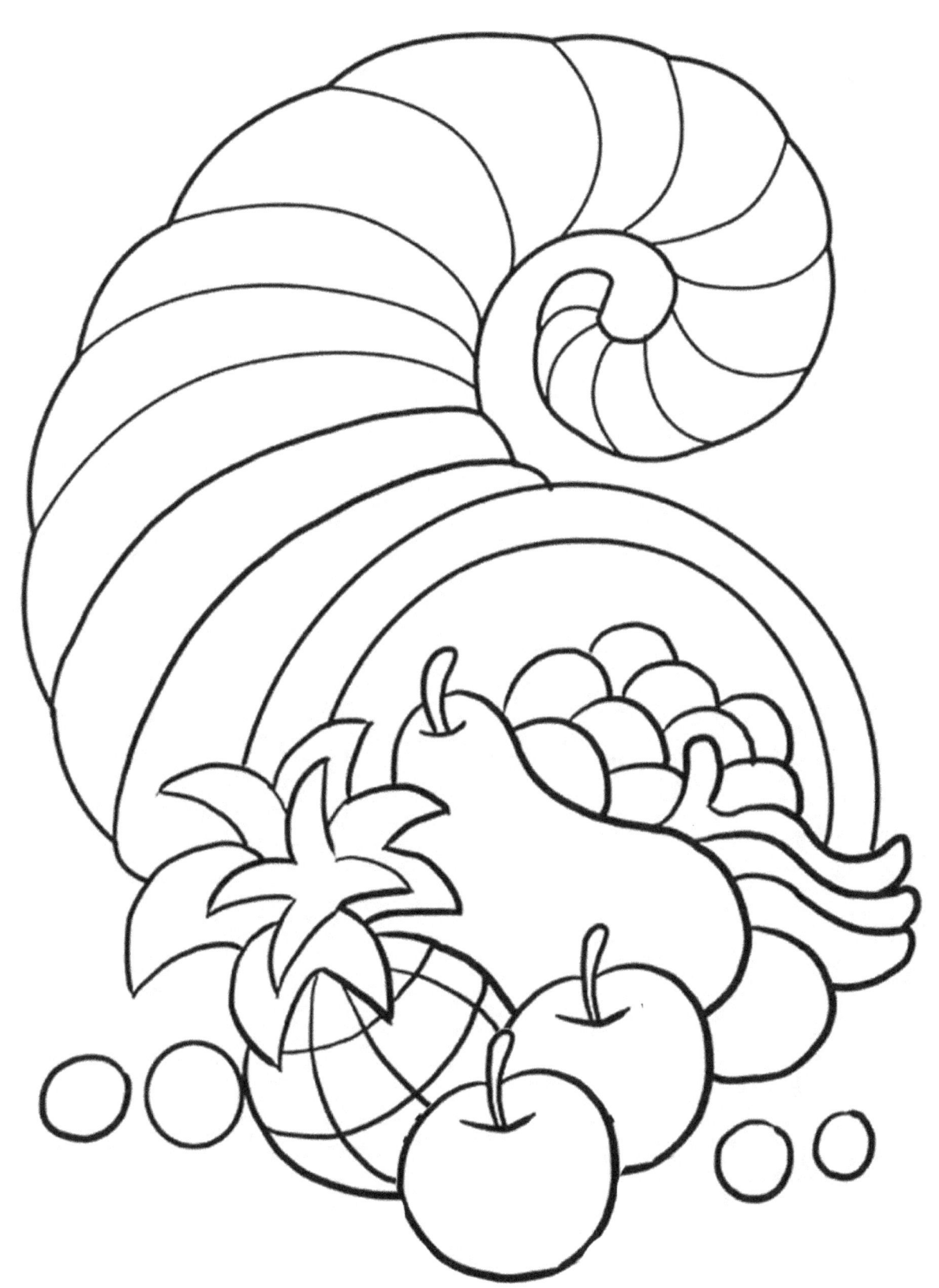

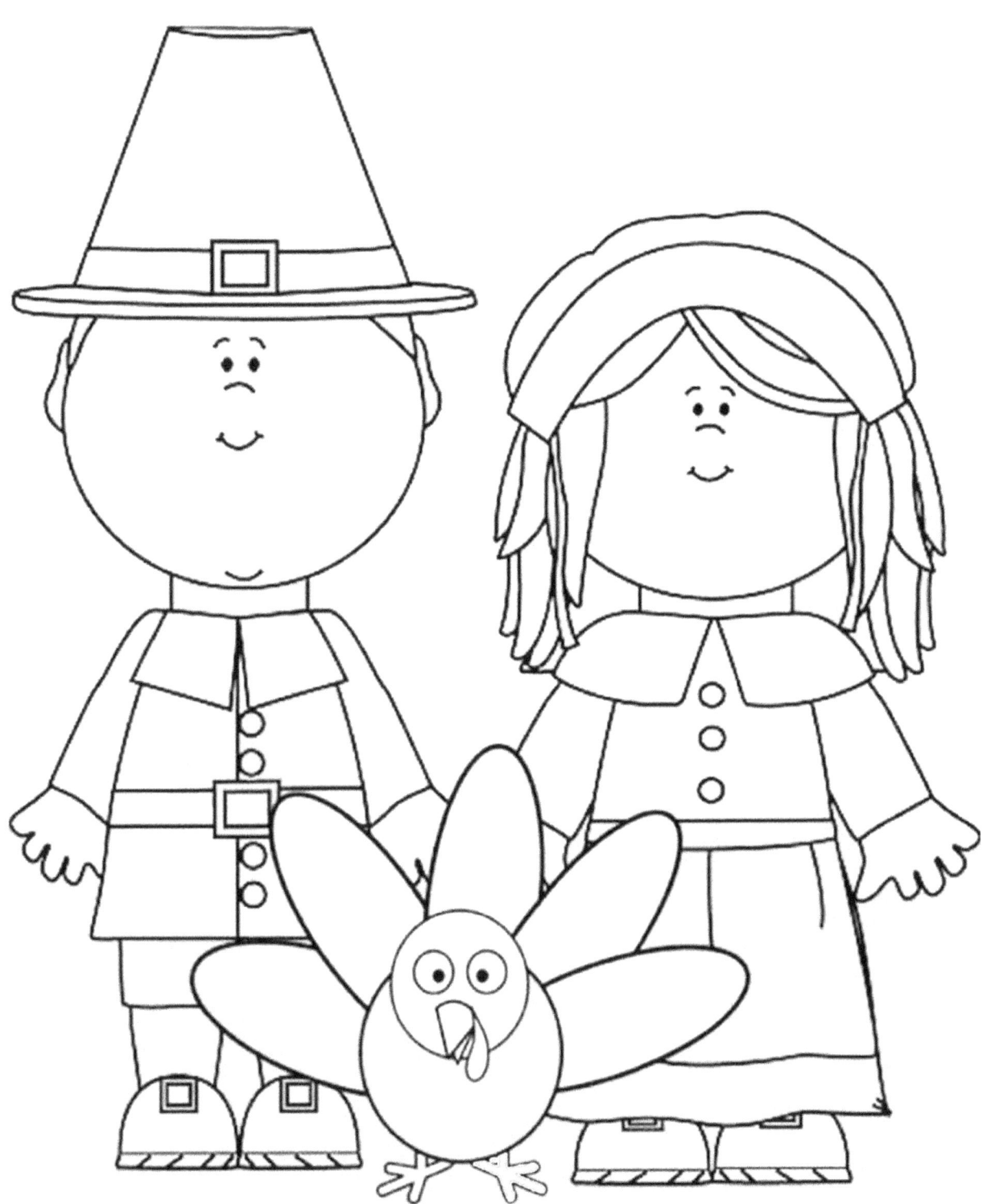

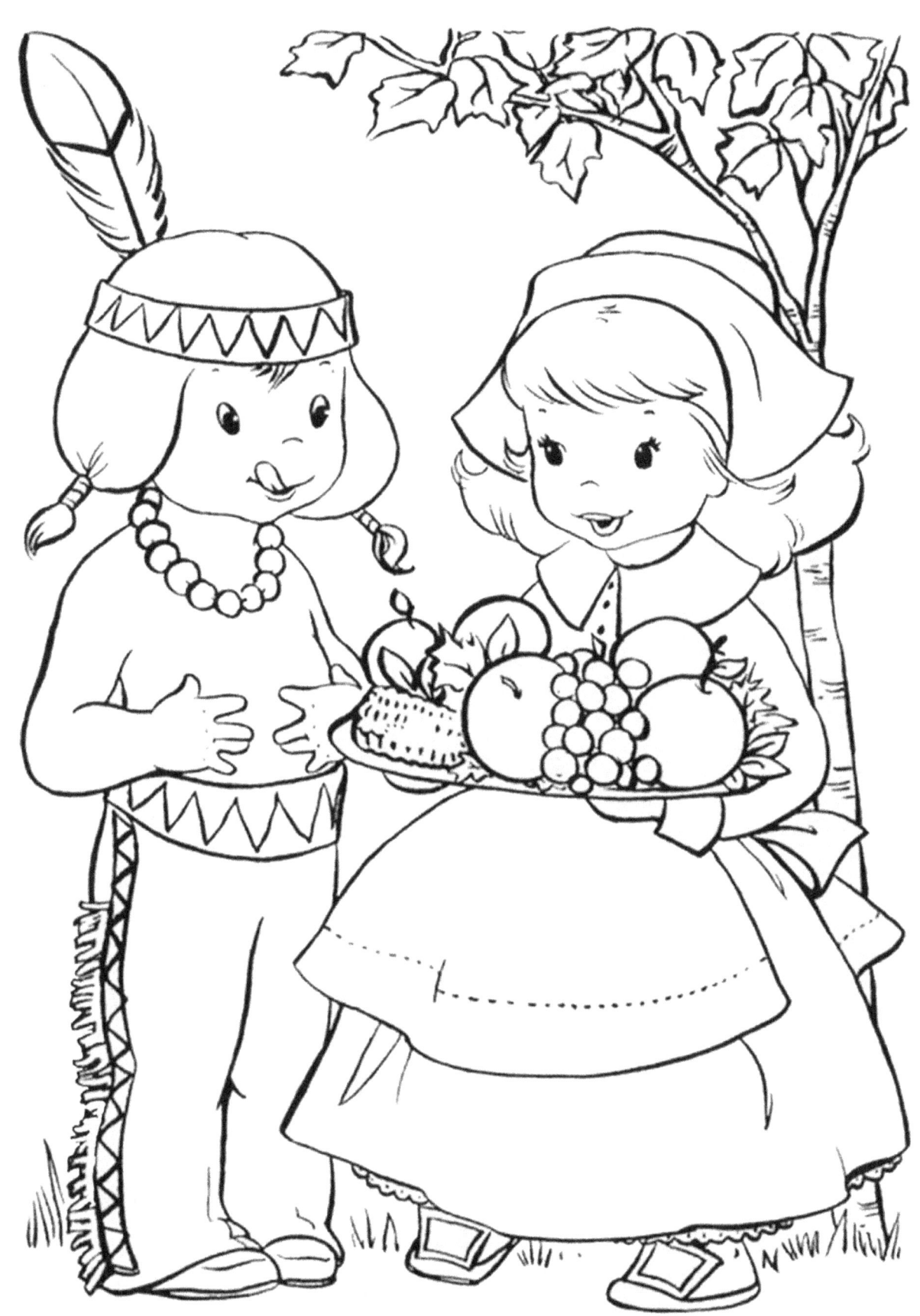

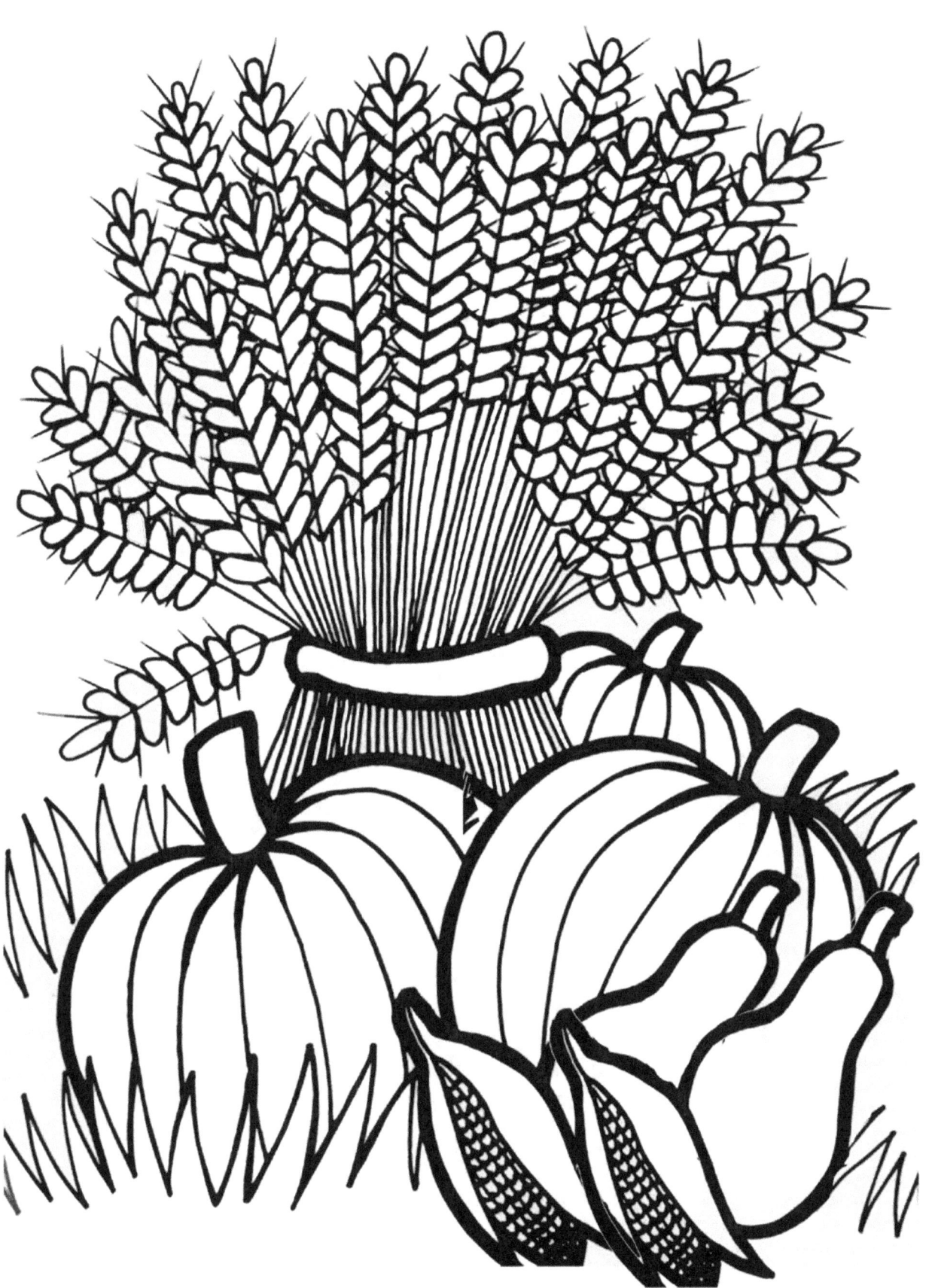

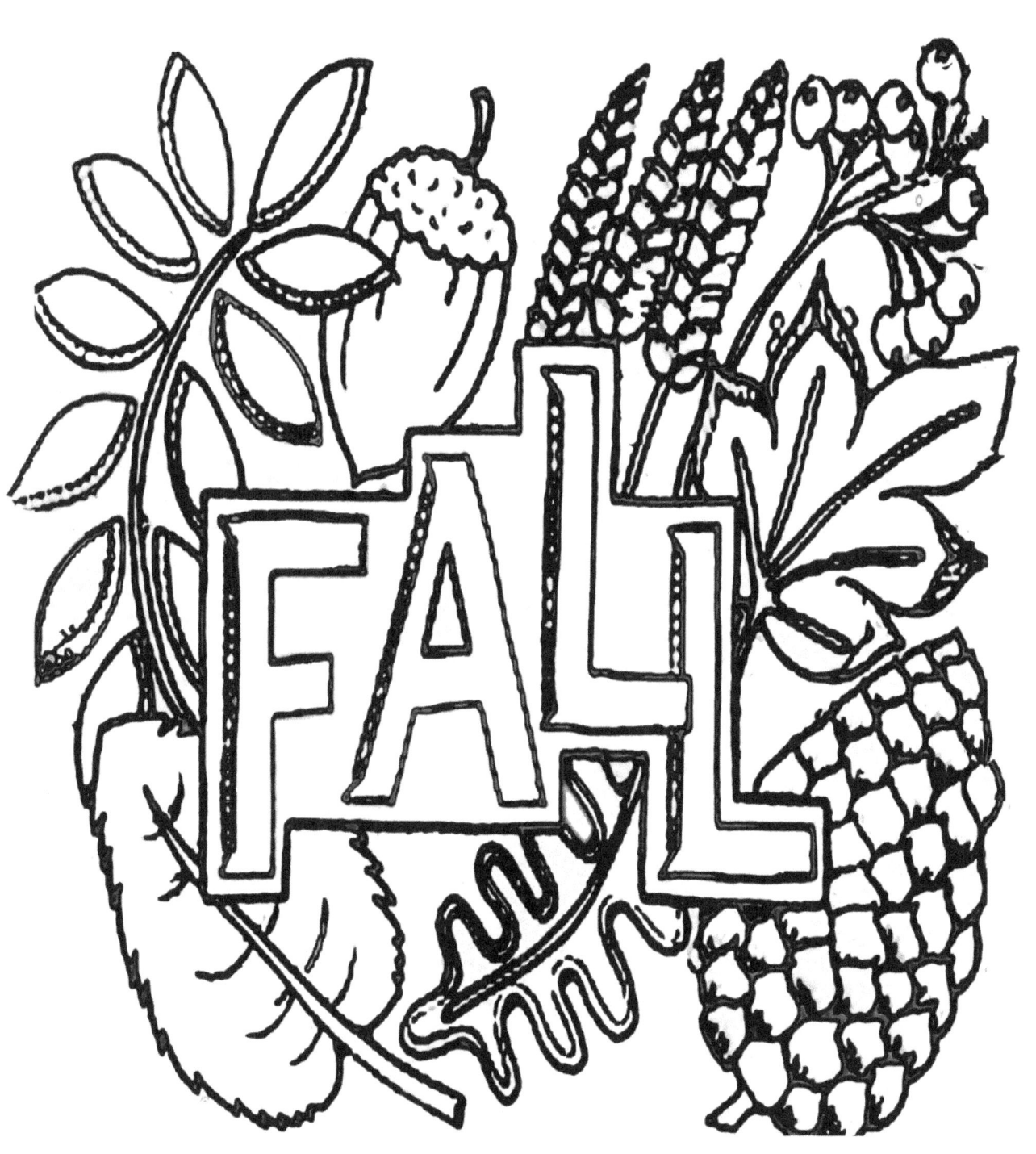

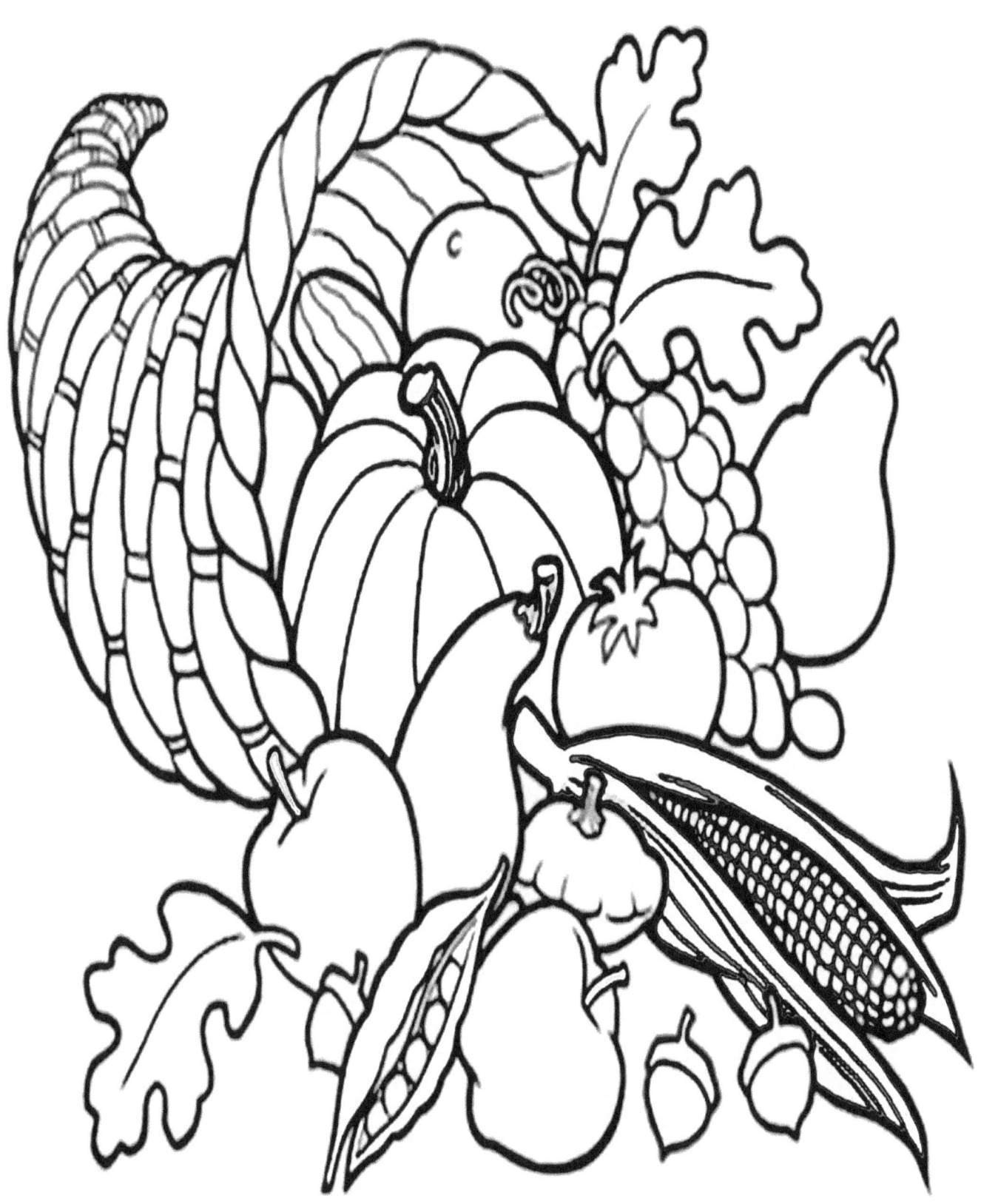

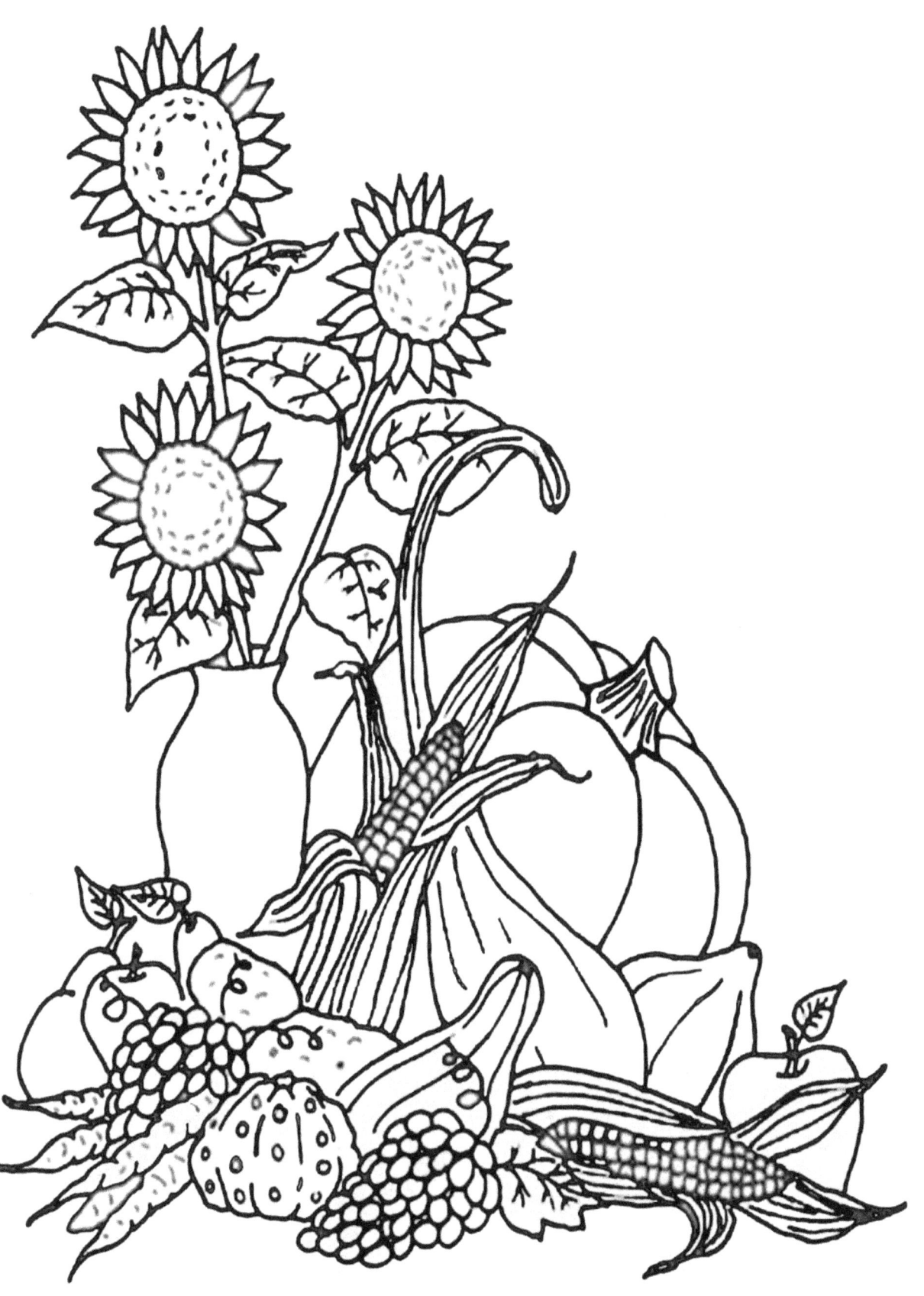

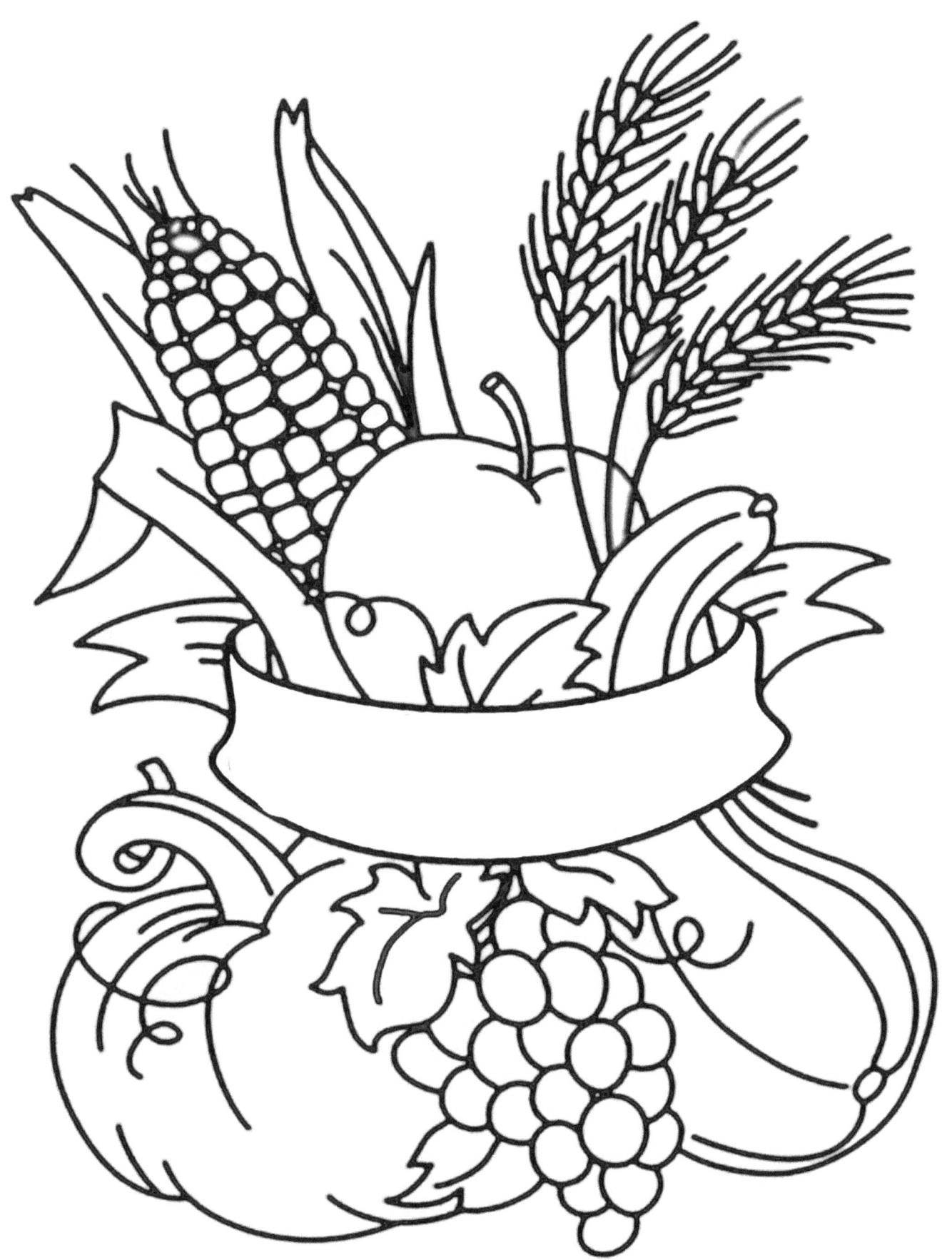

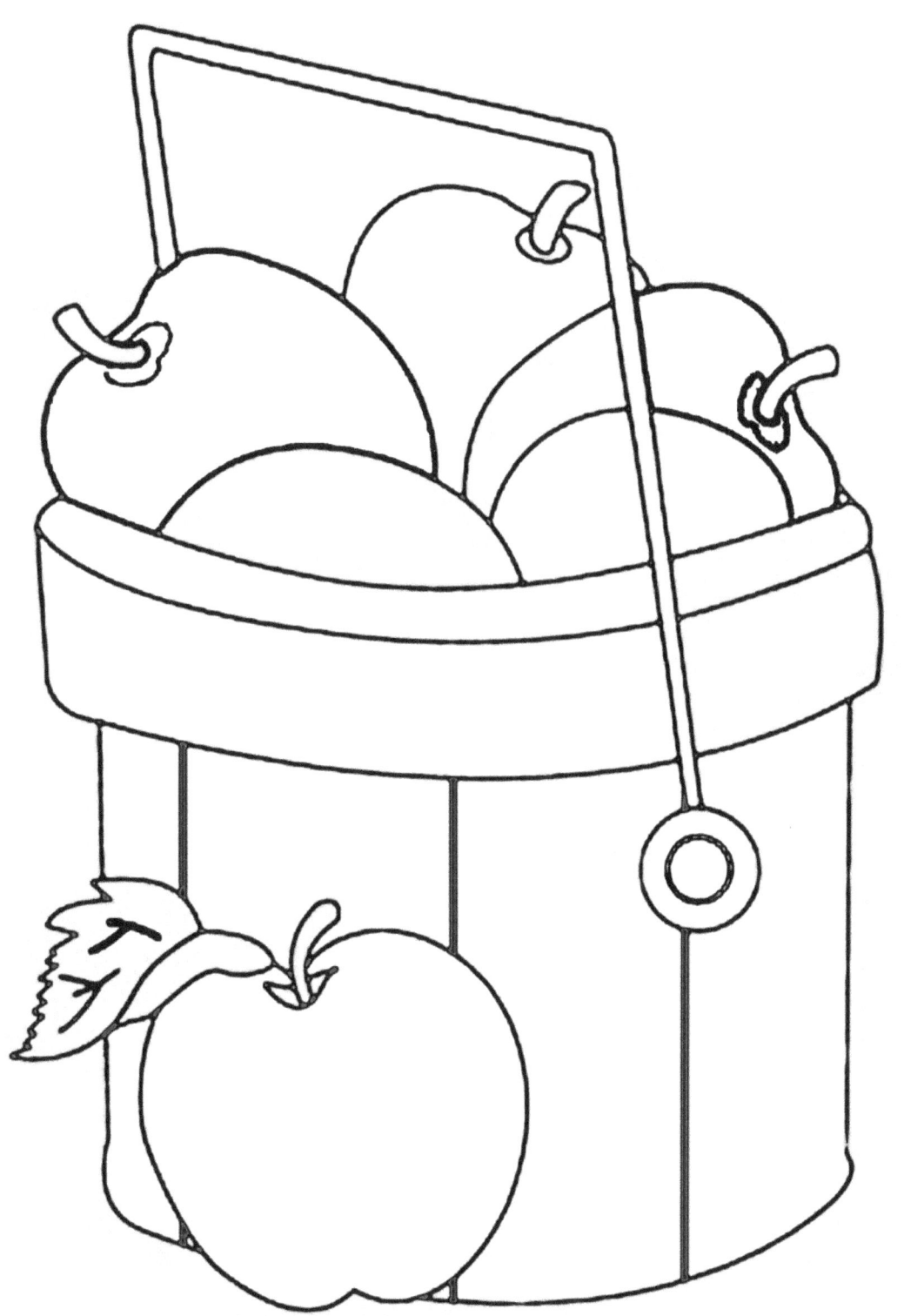

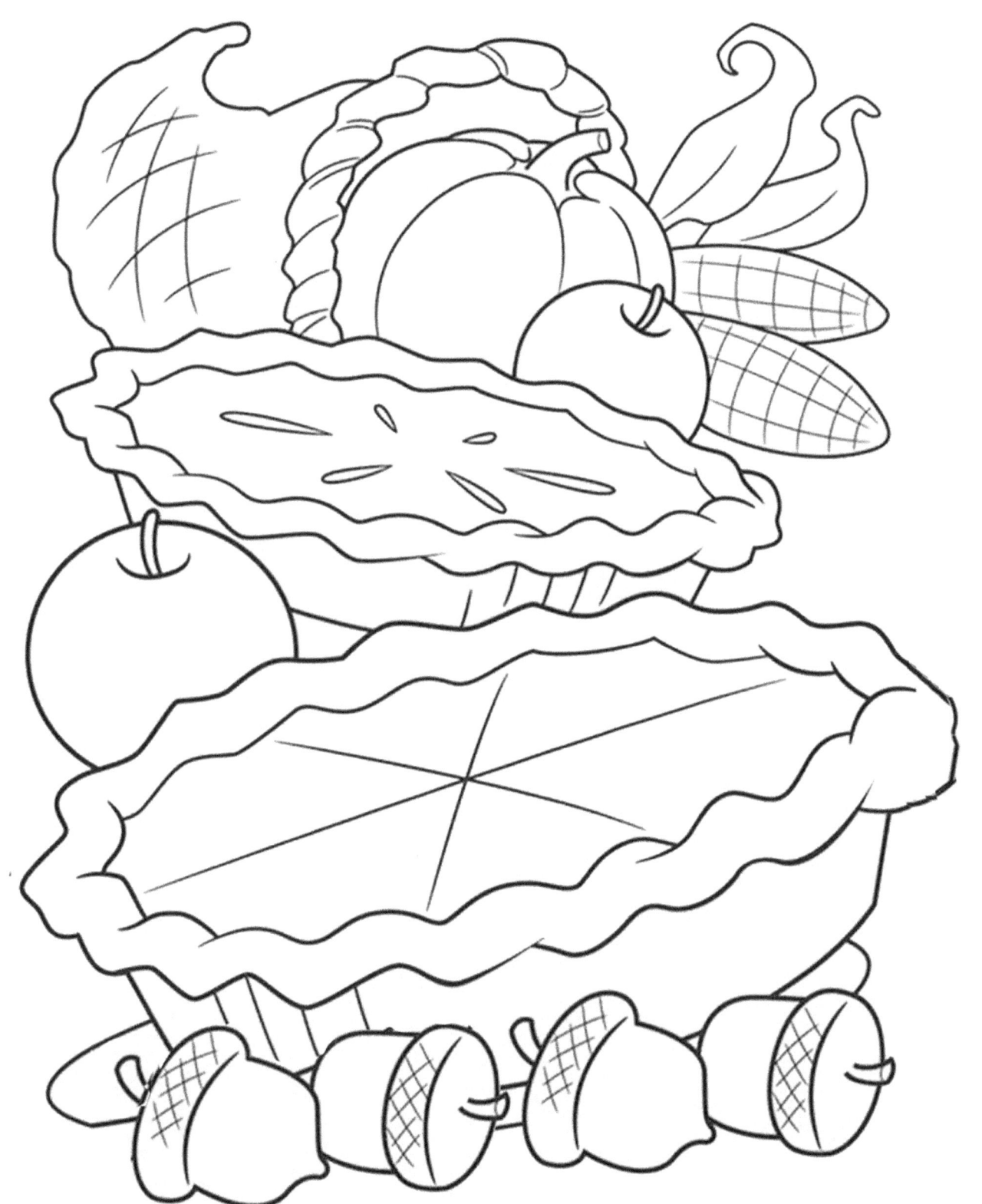

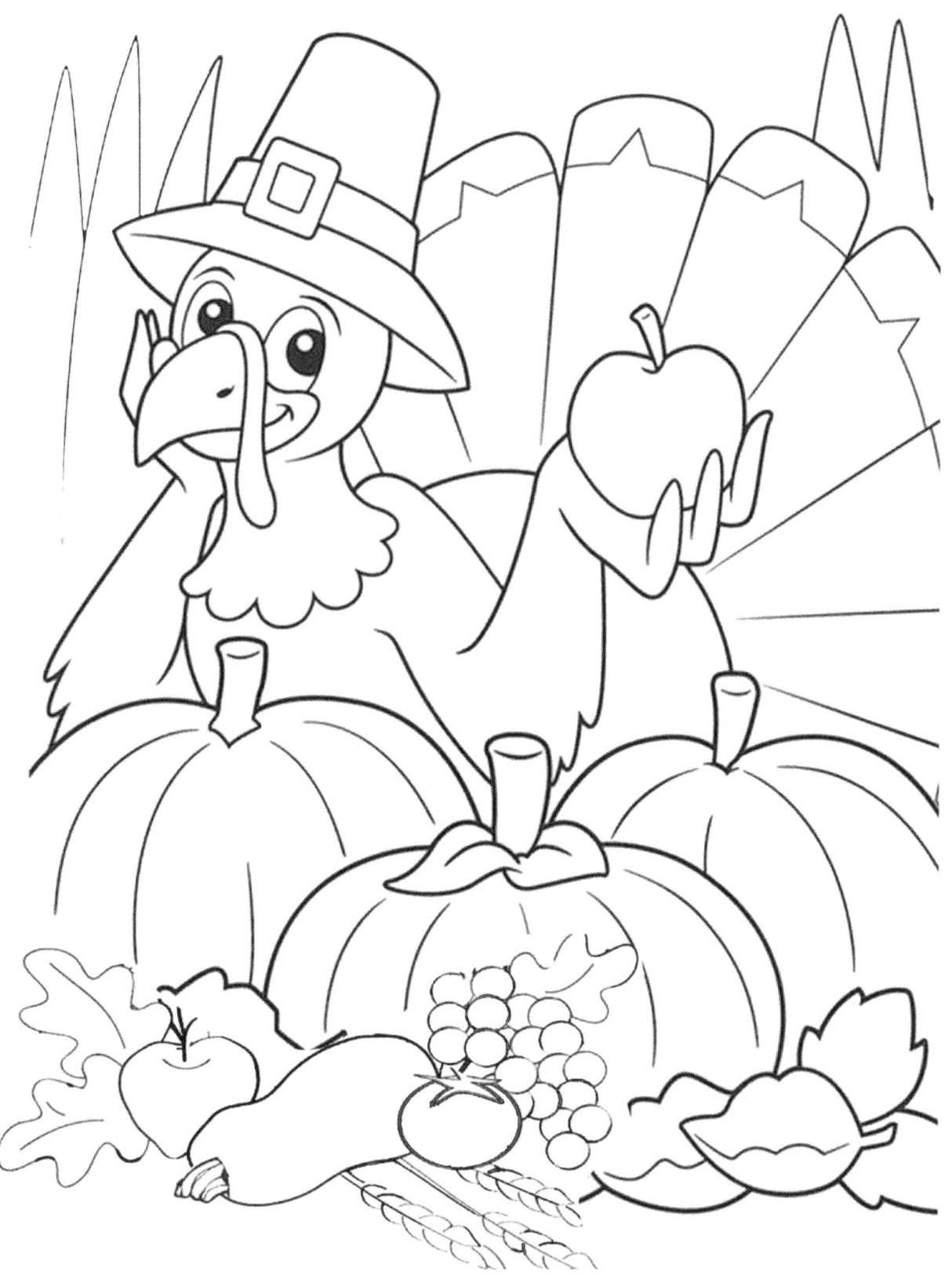

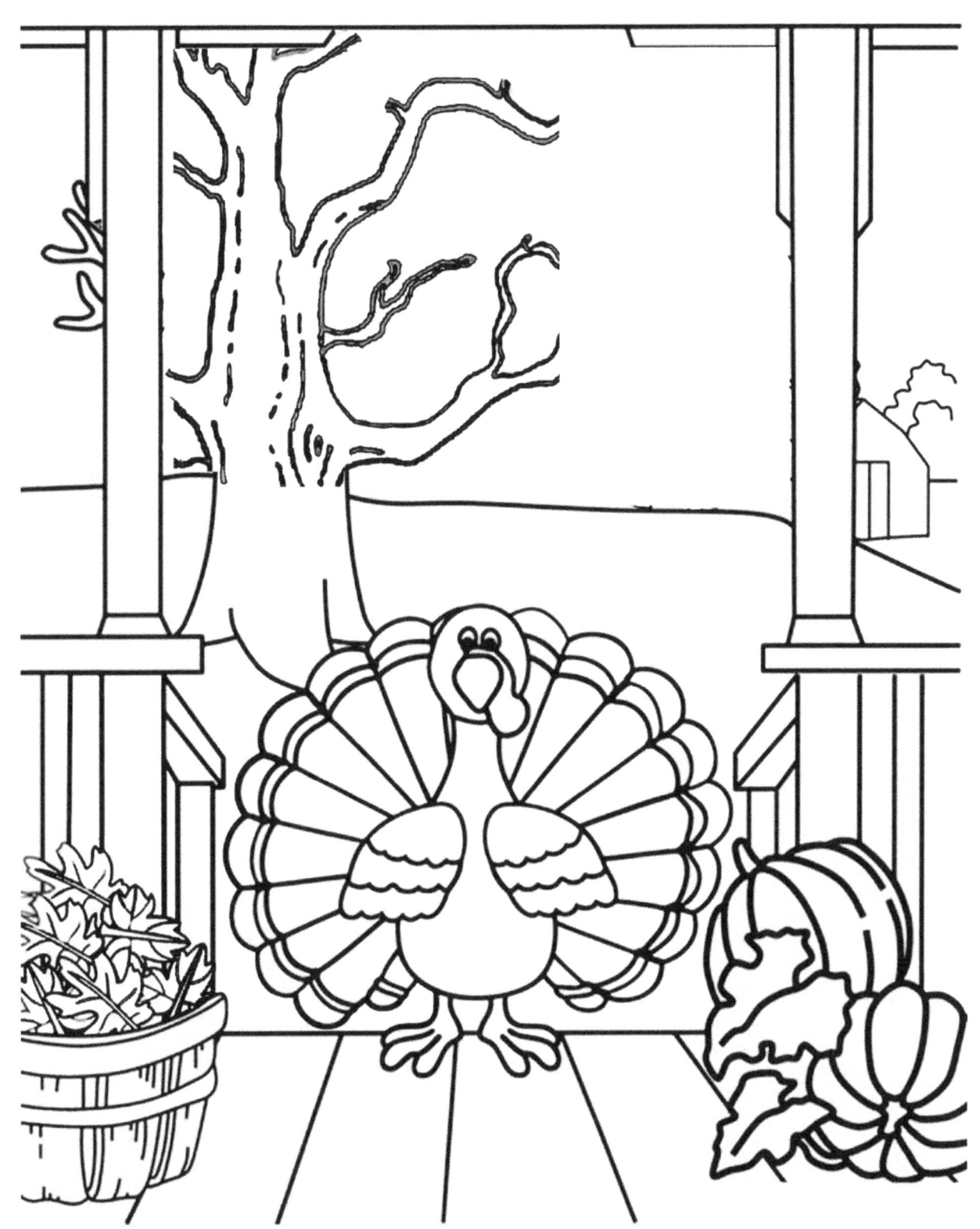

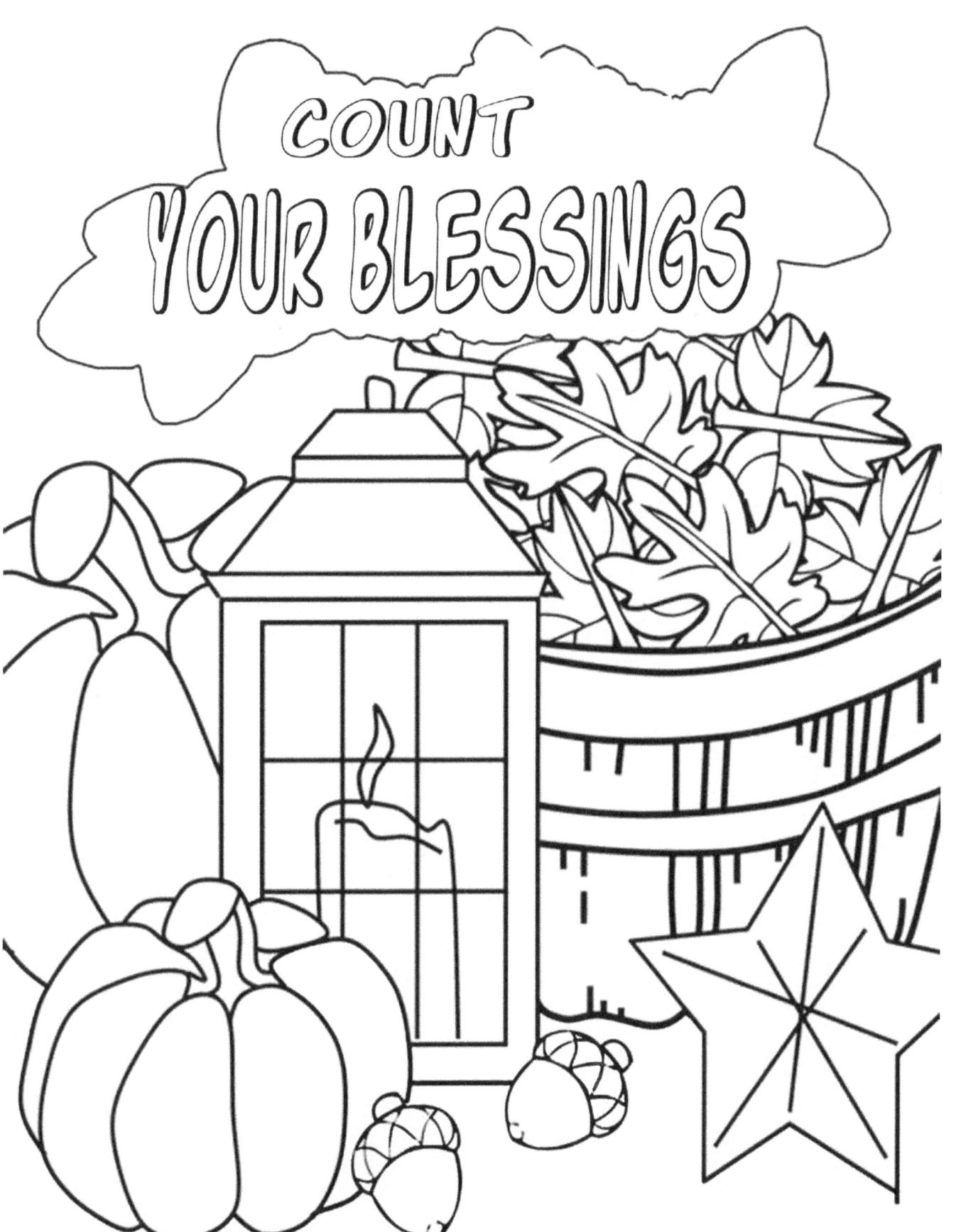

I AM THANKFUL FOR GOD BLESING

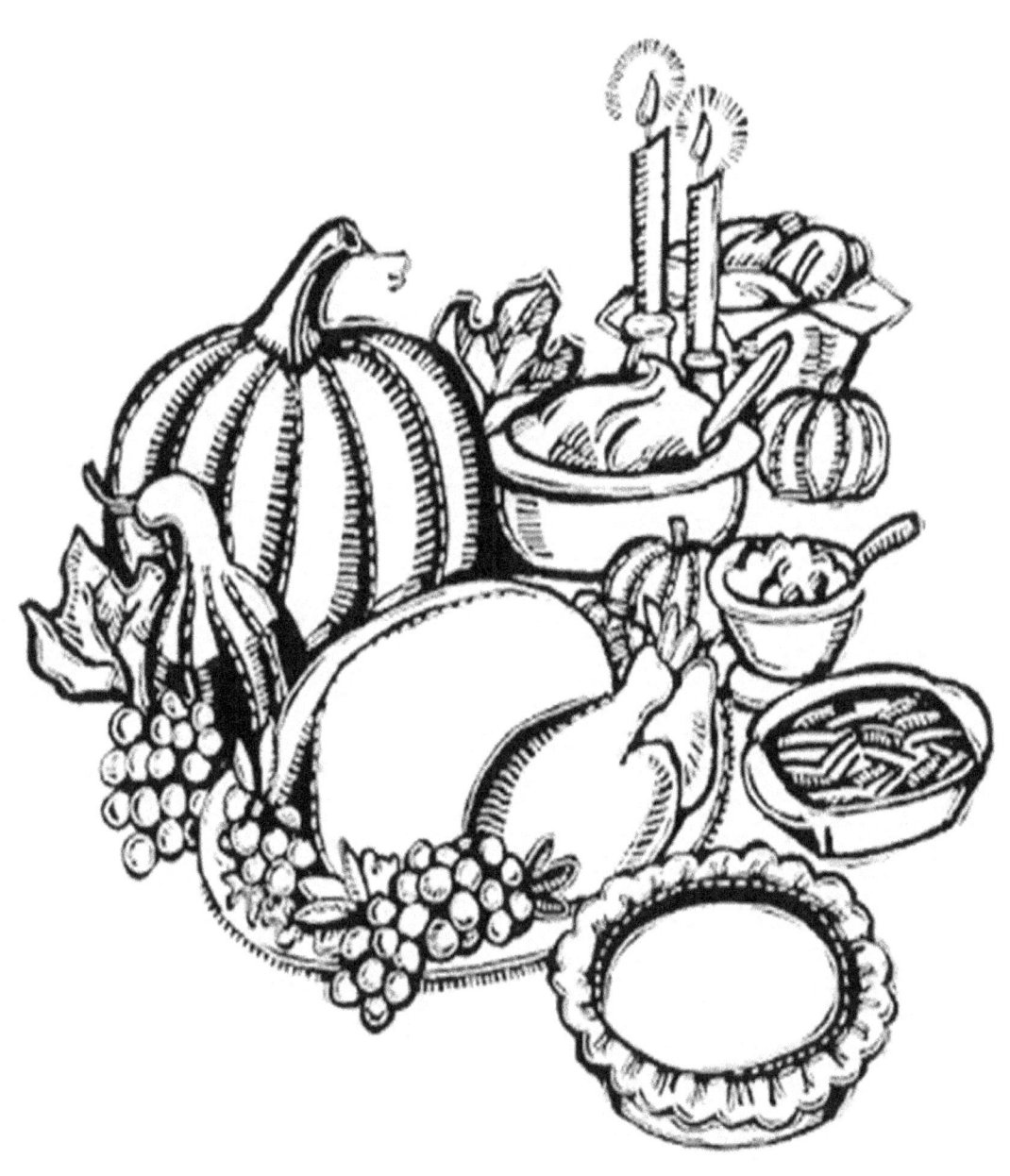

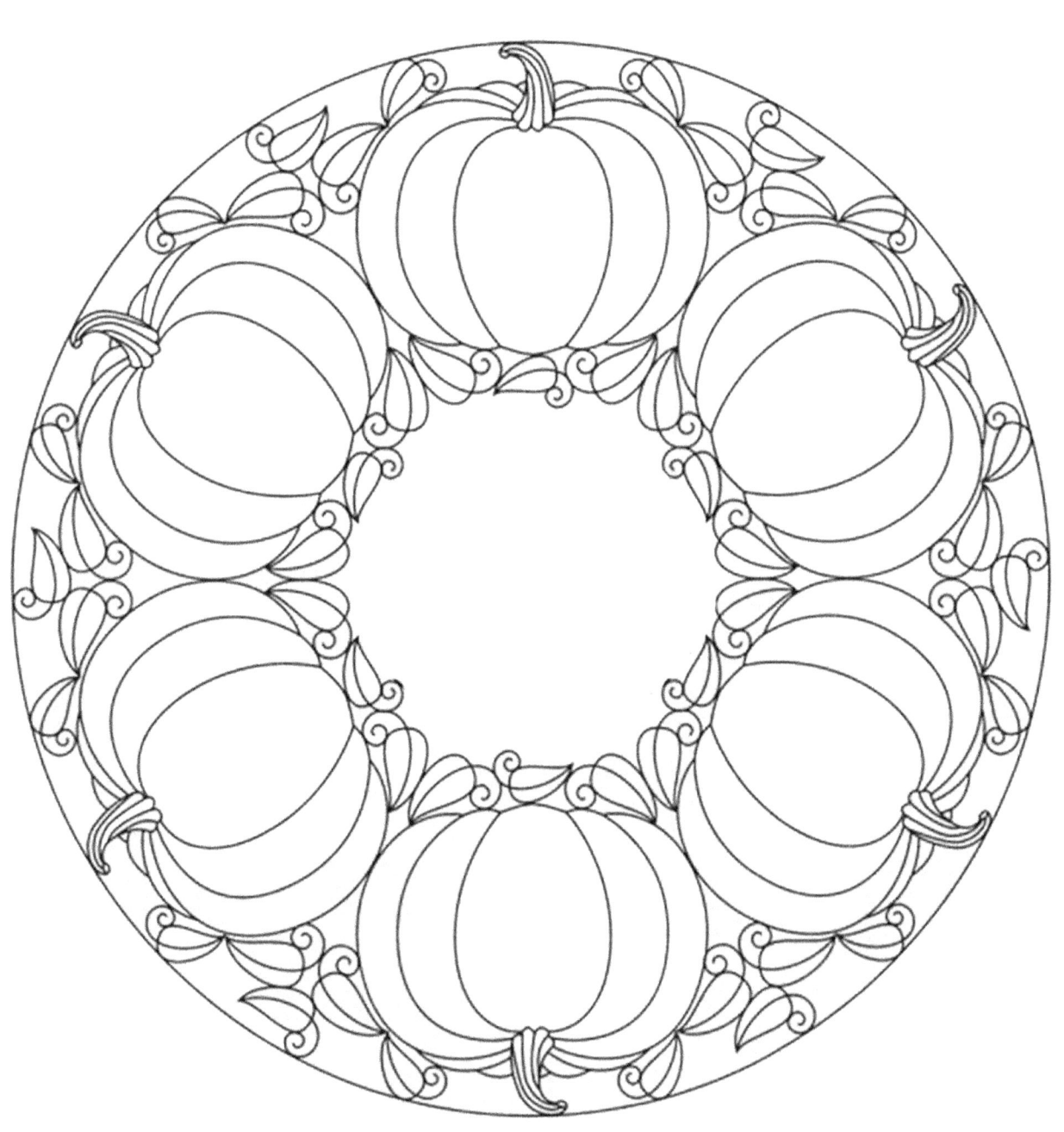

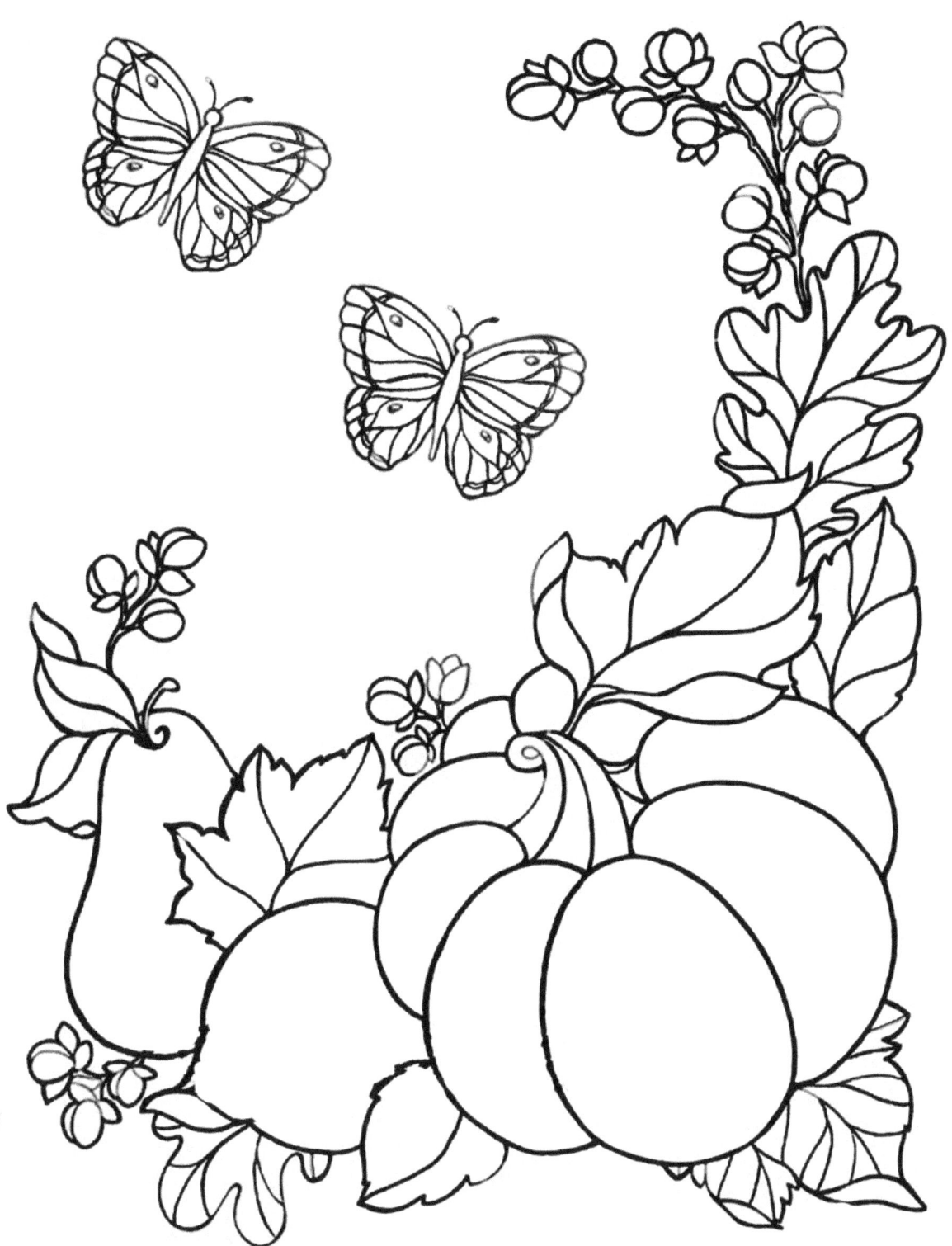

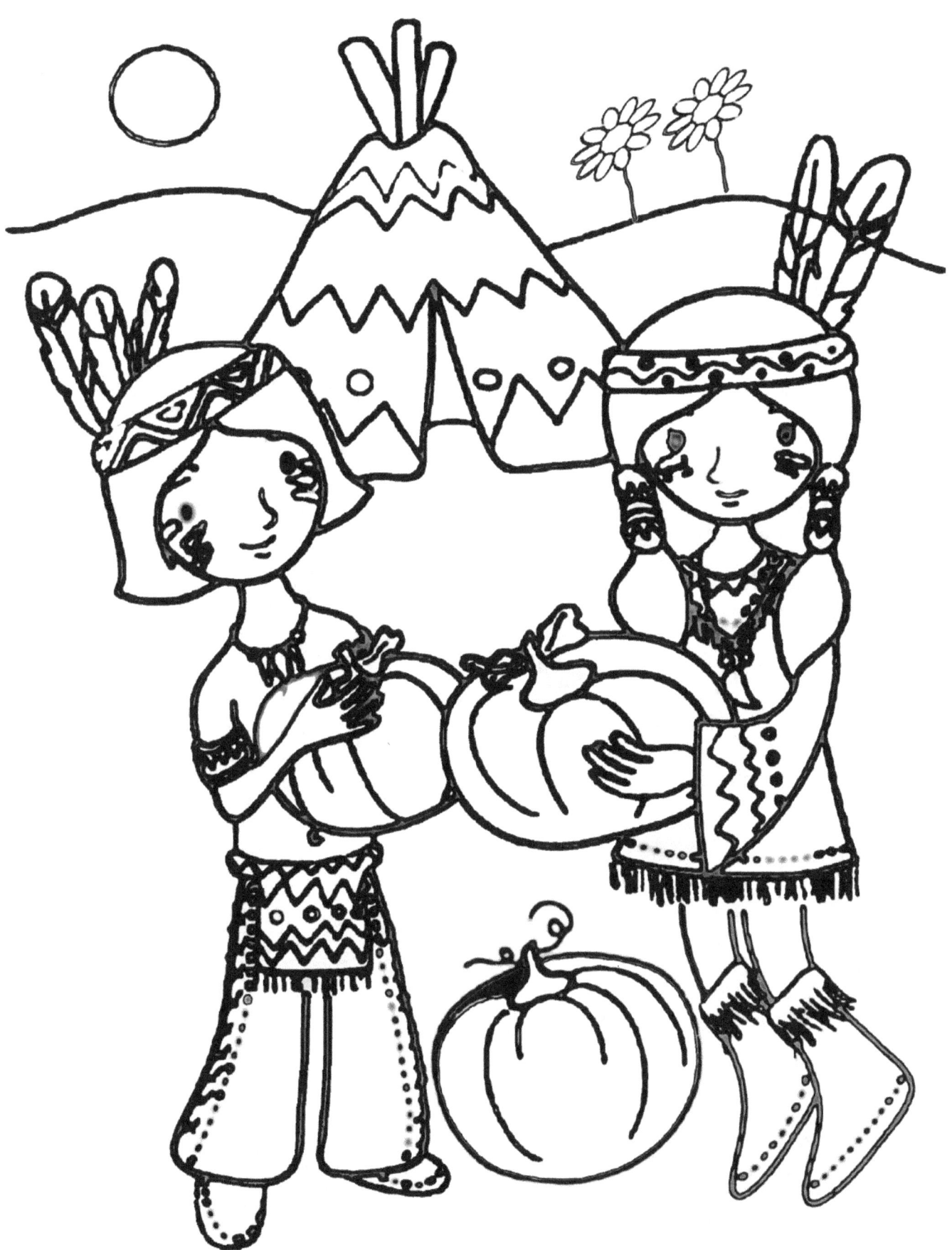

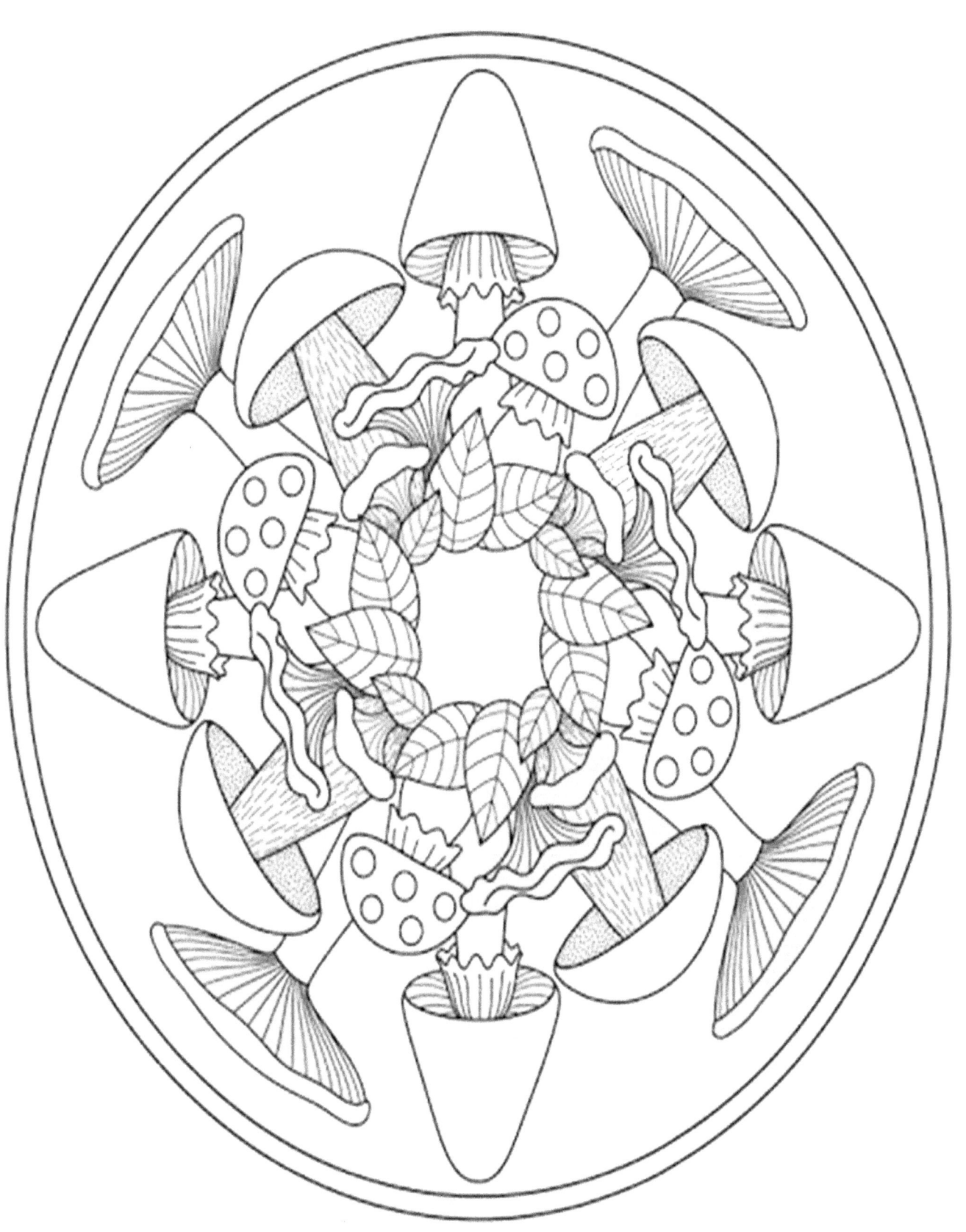

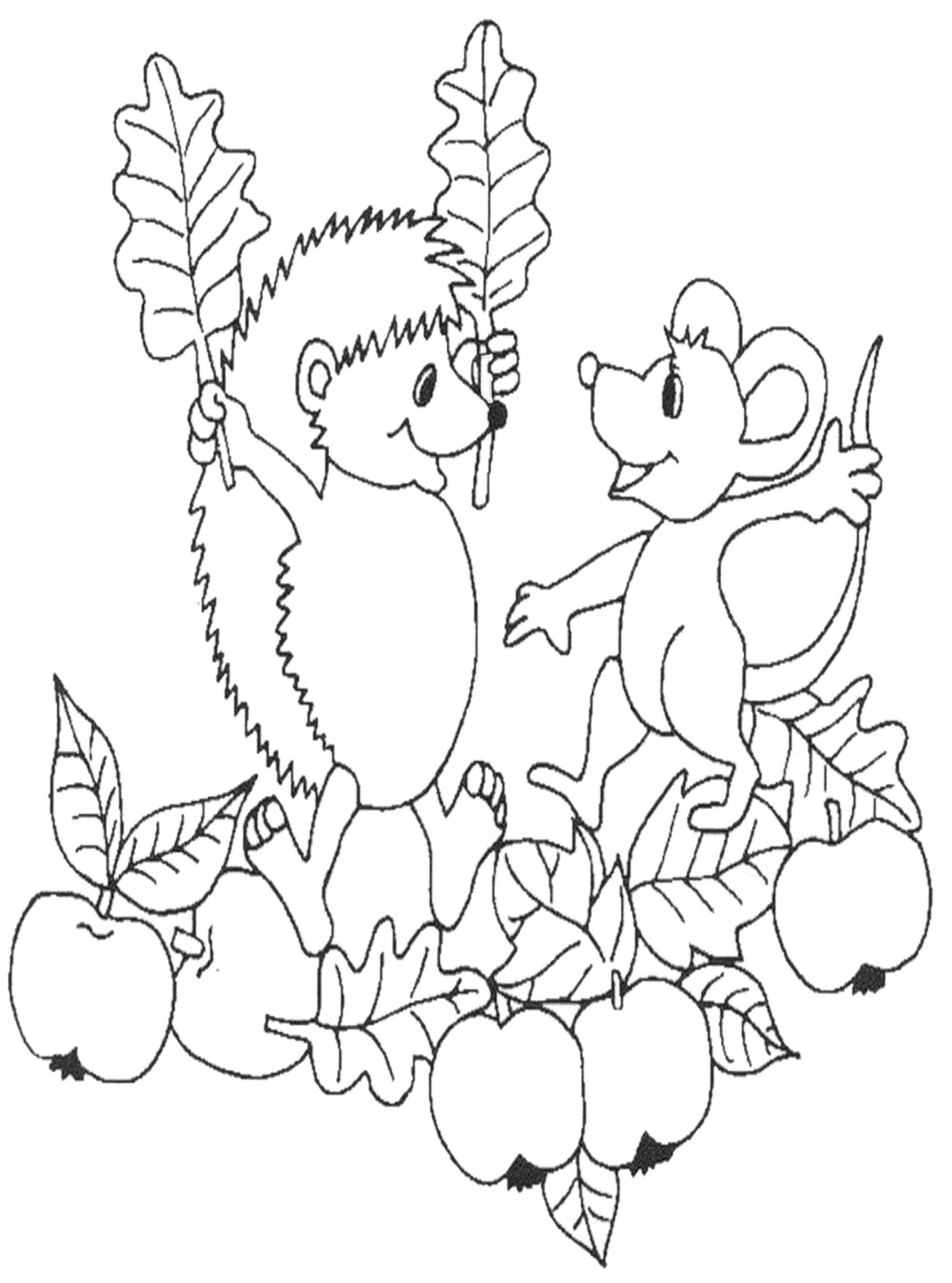

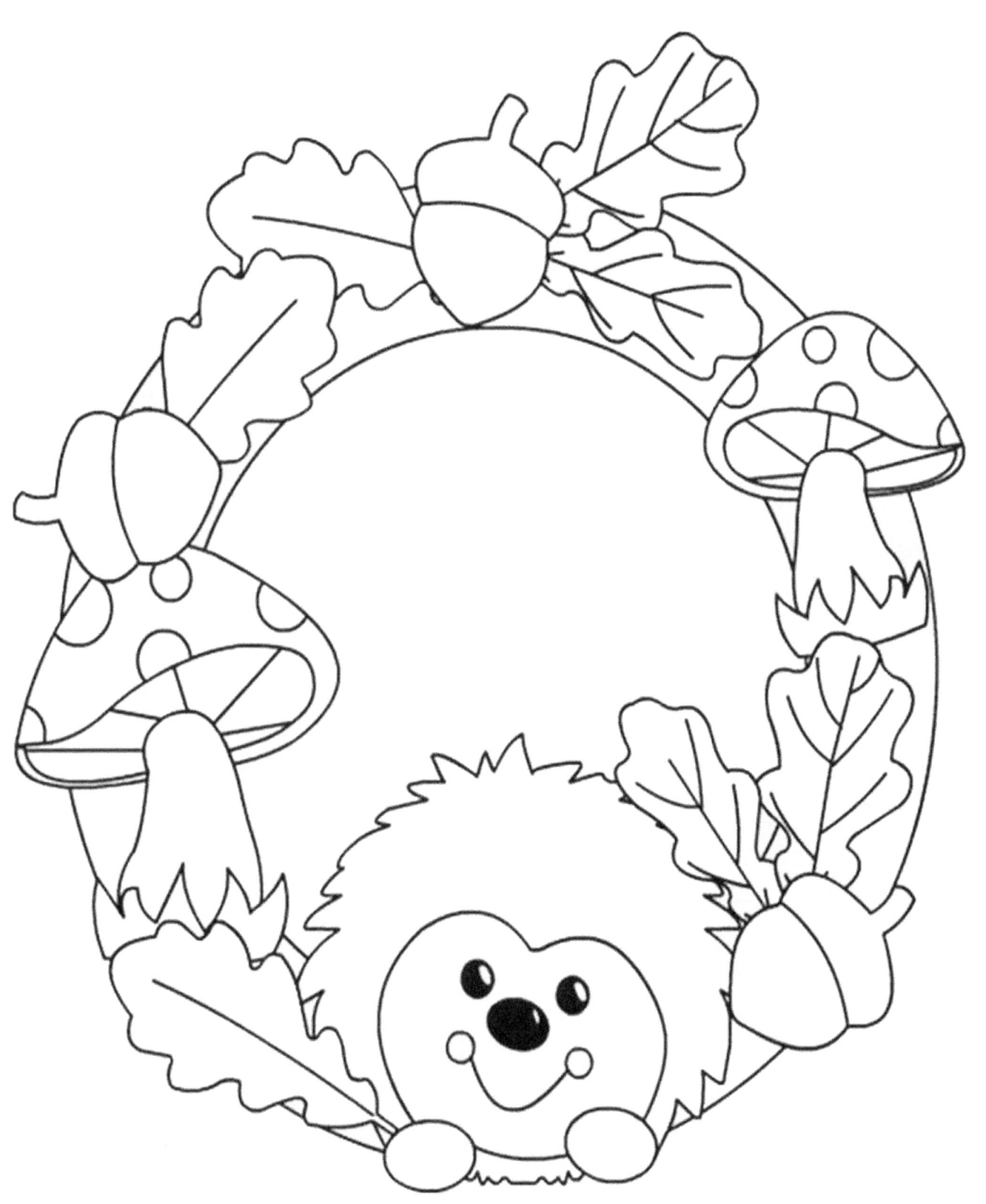

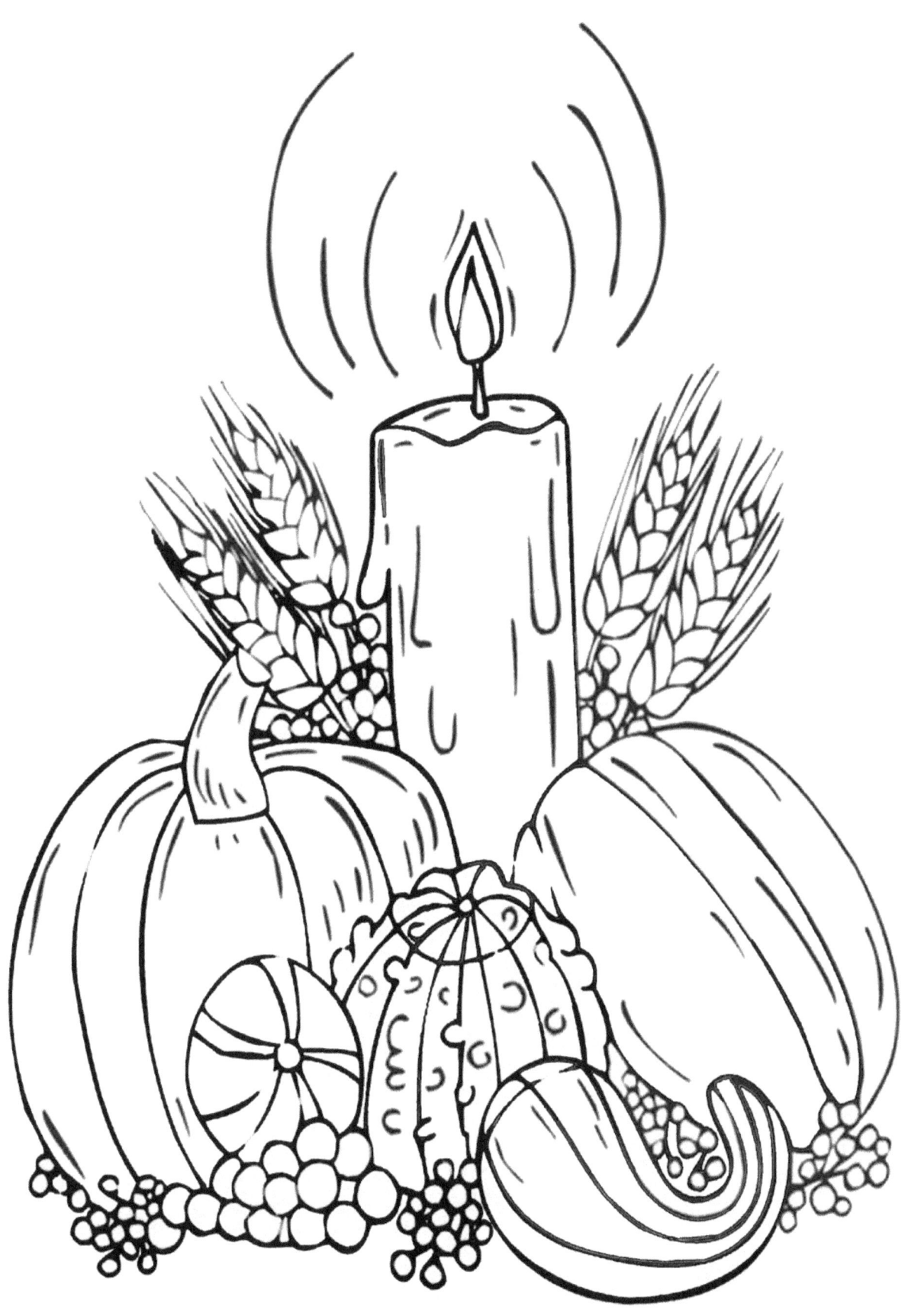

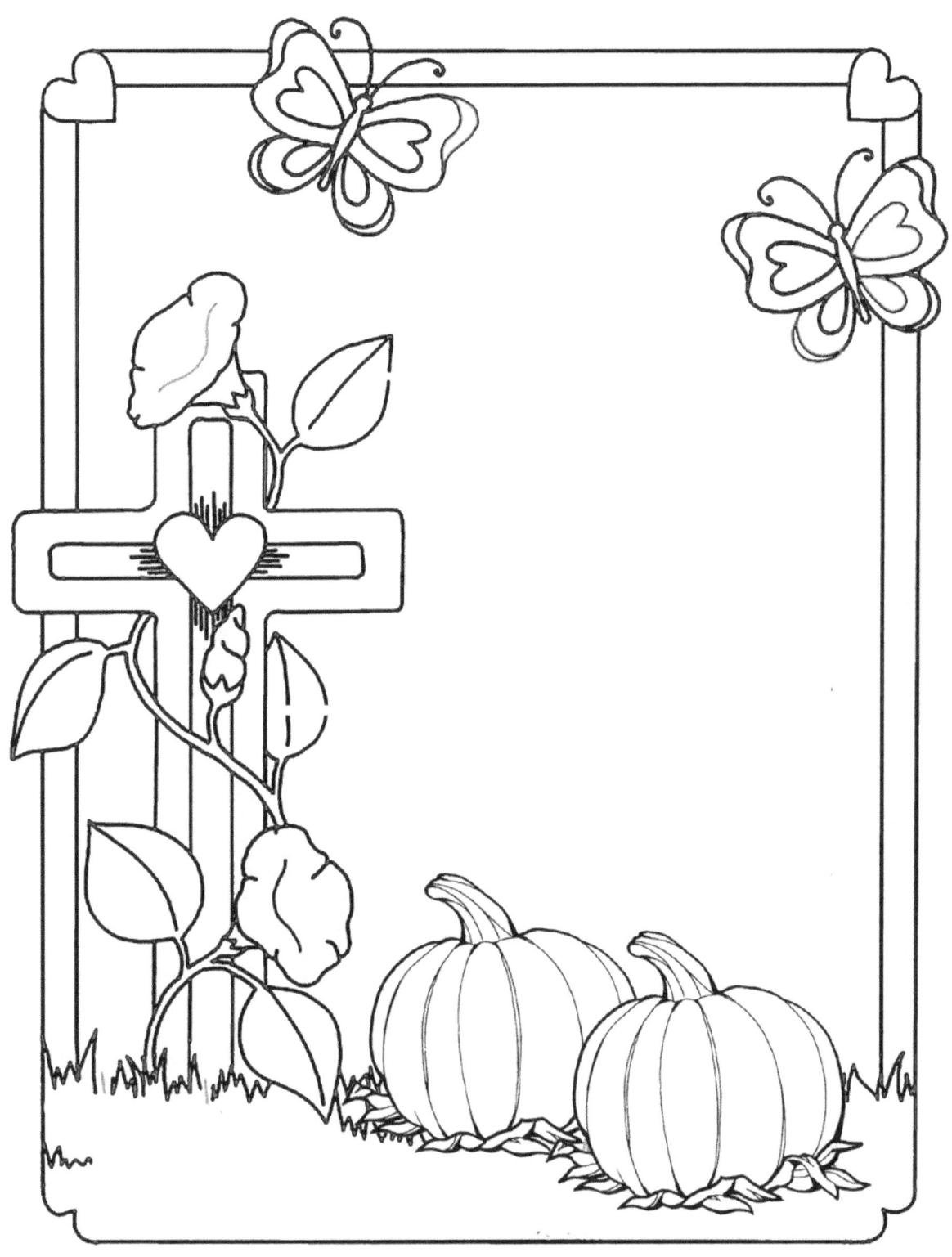

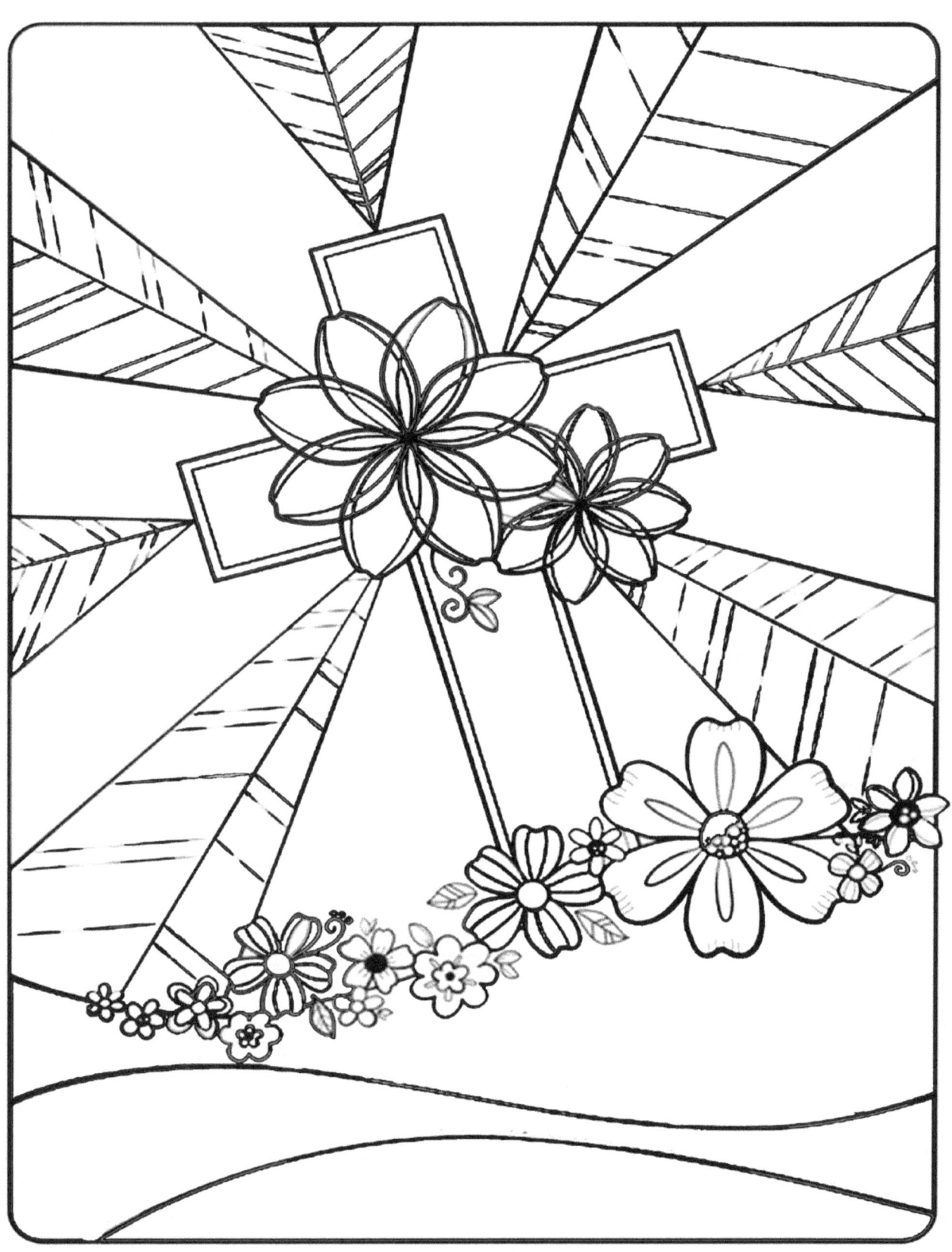

AUTUMN TREE

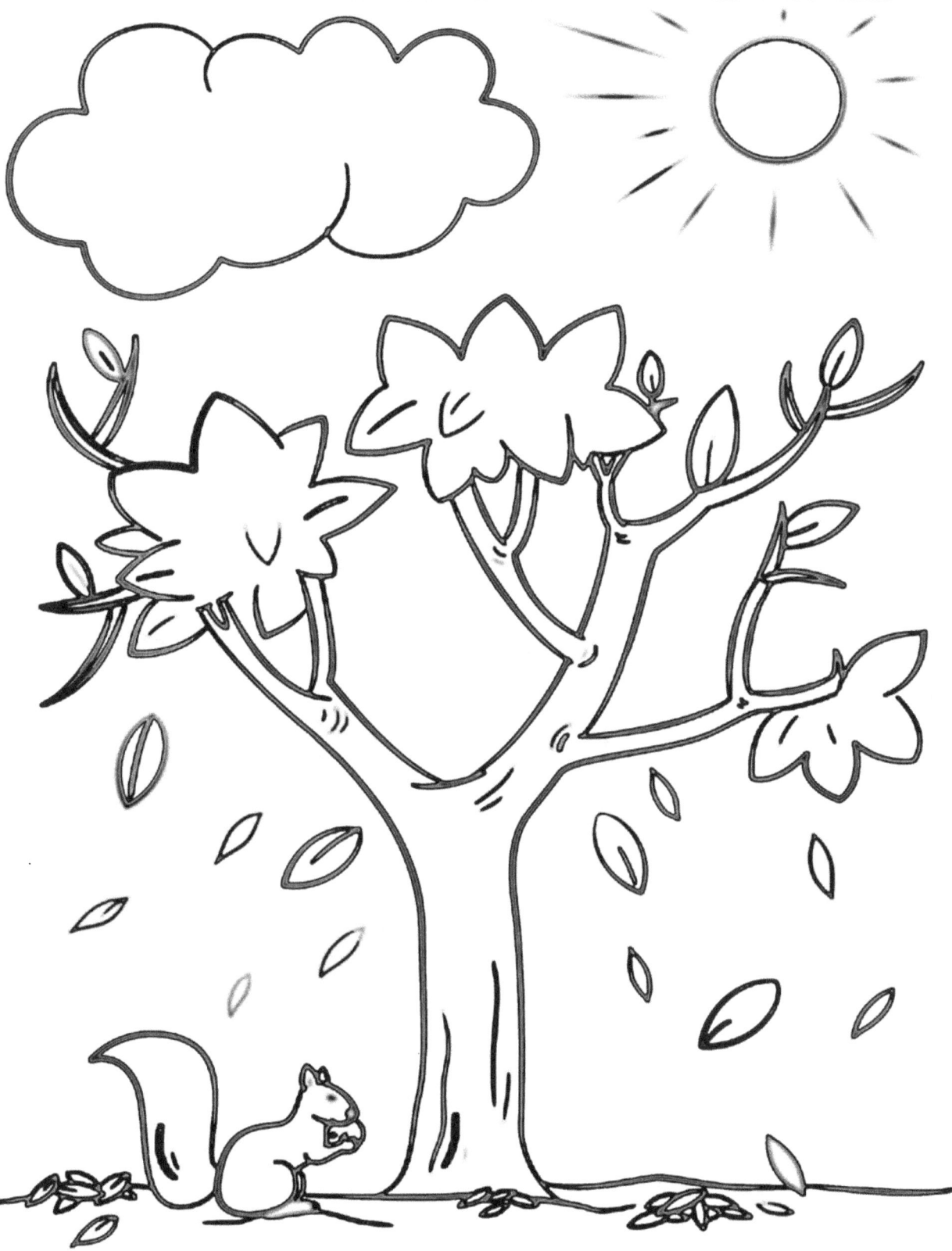

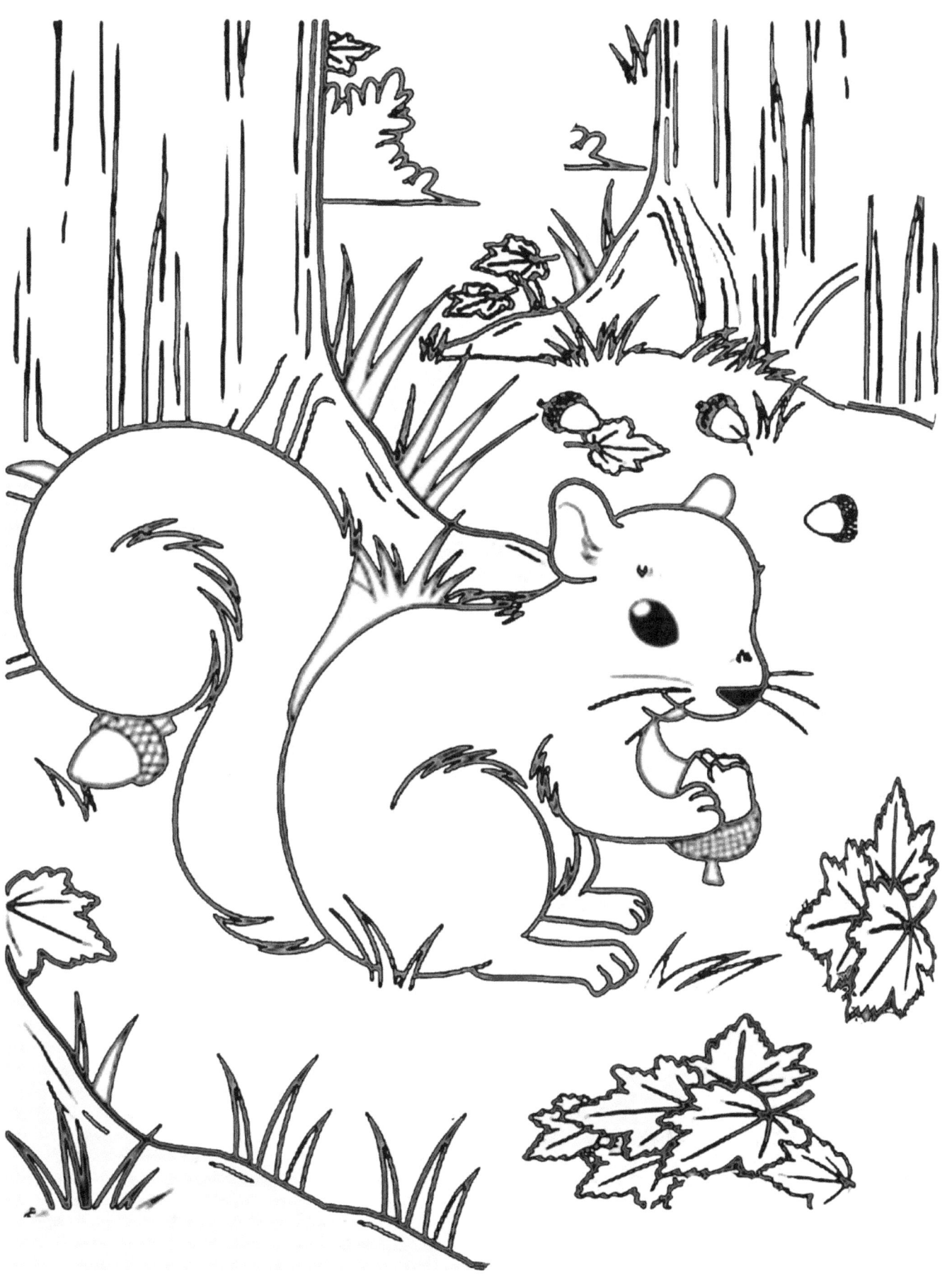

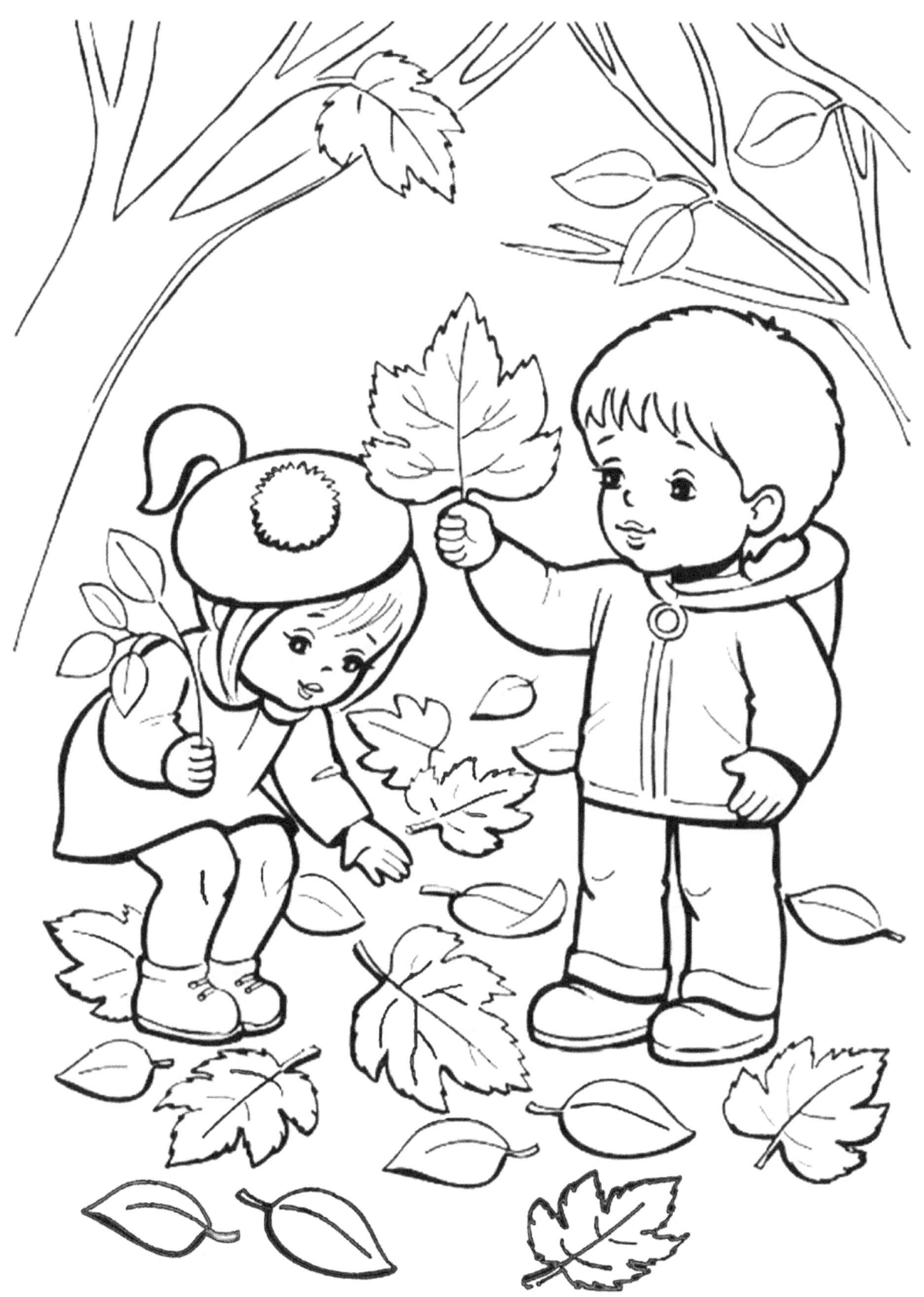

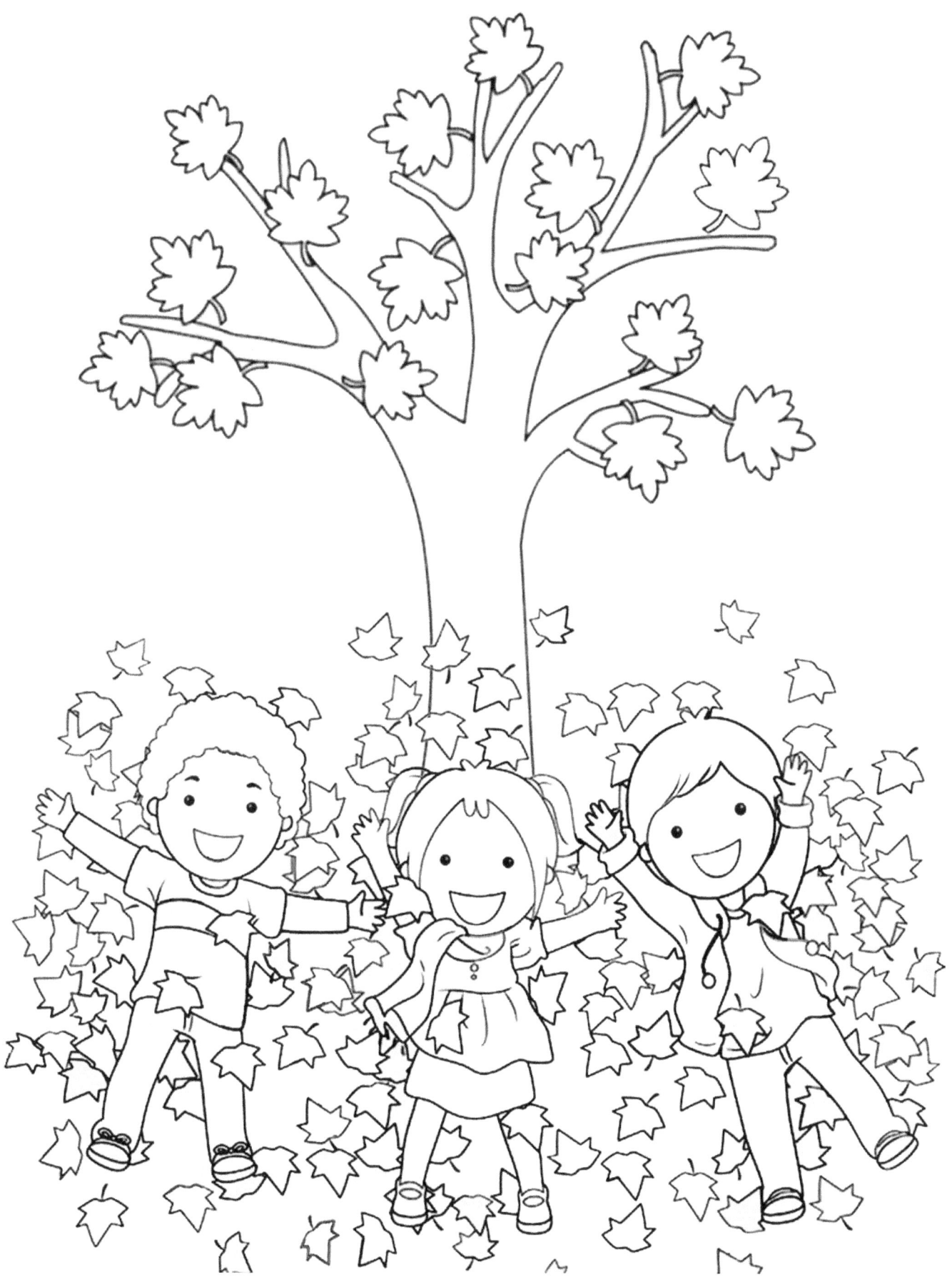

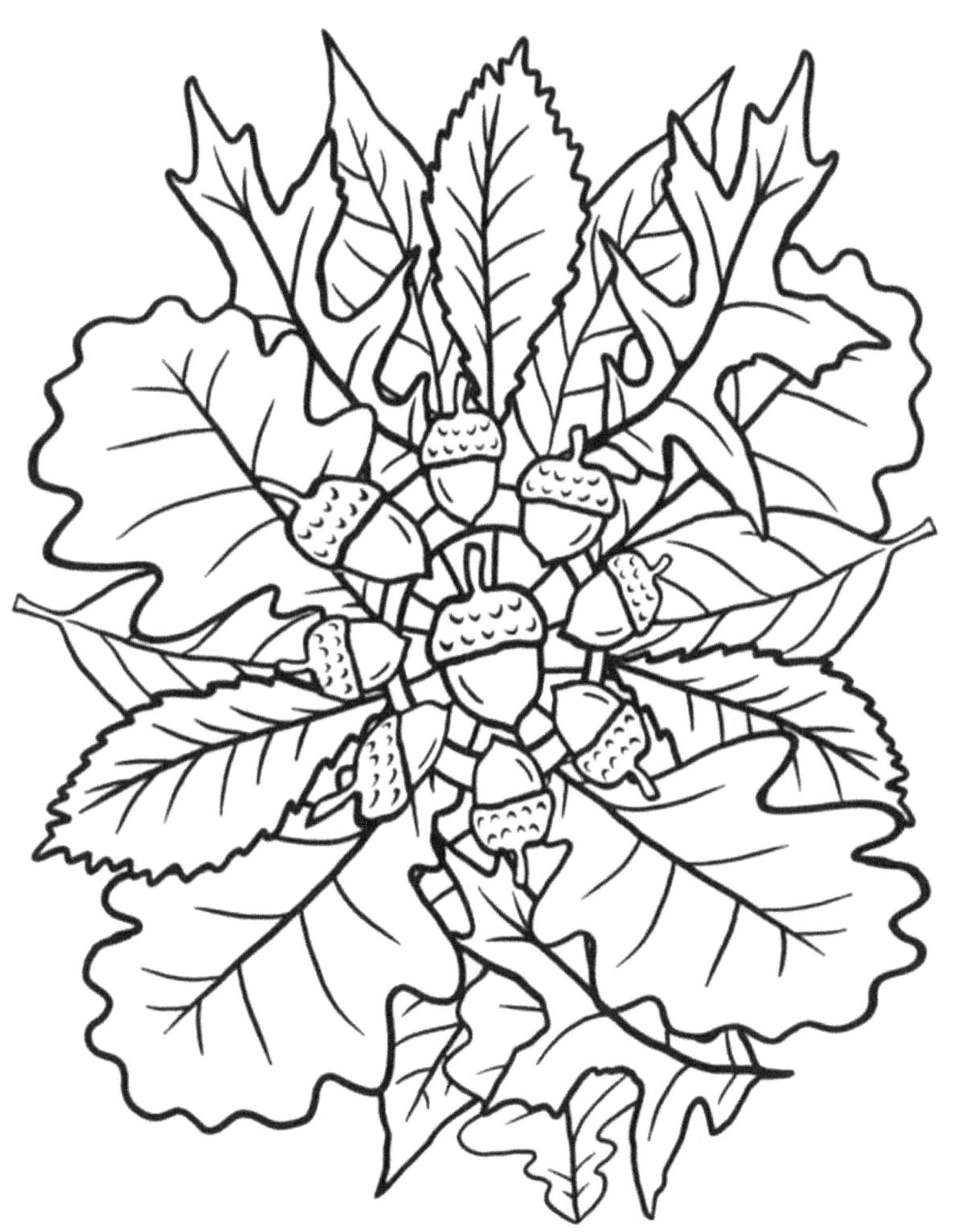

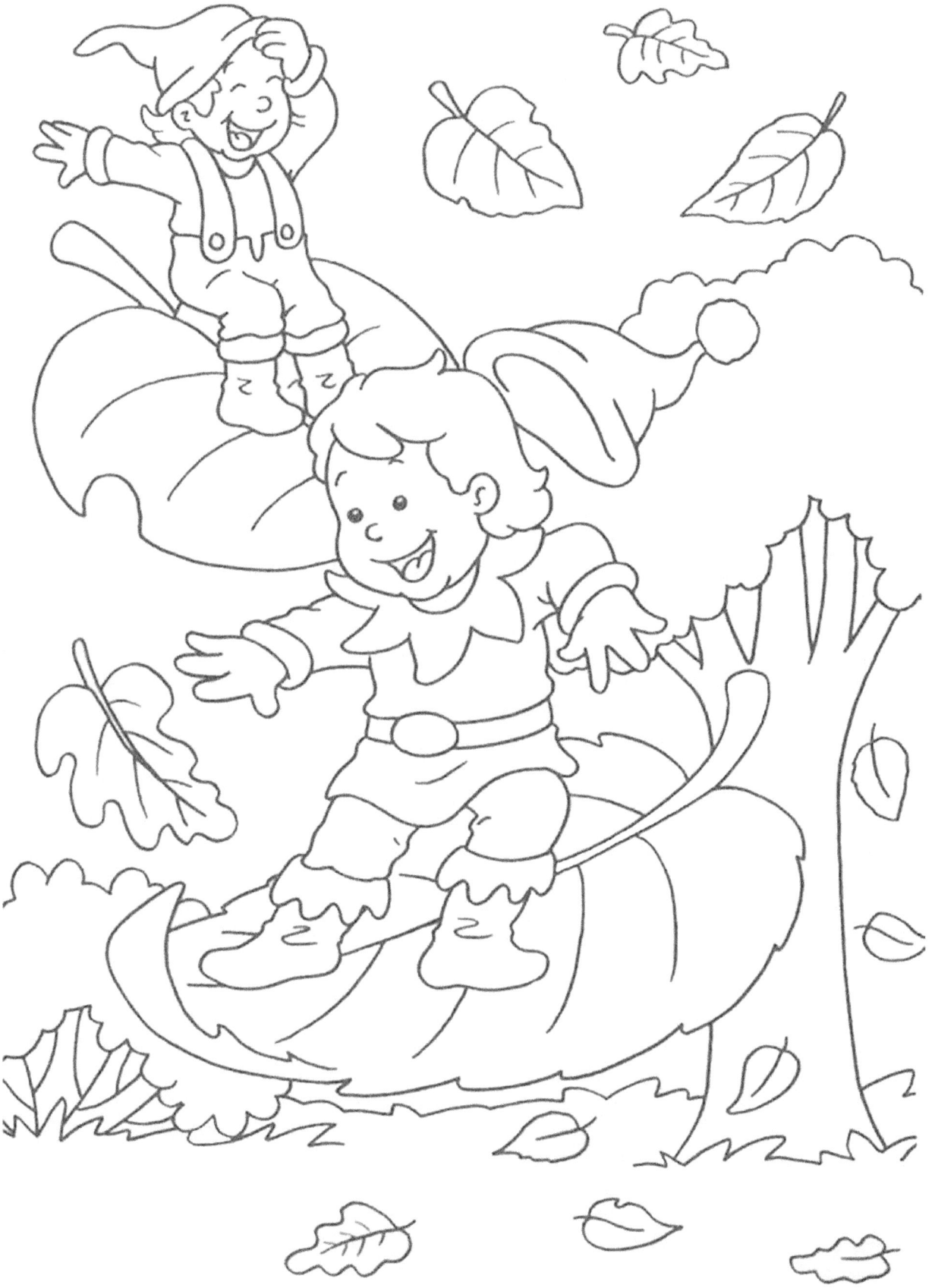

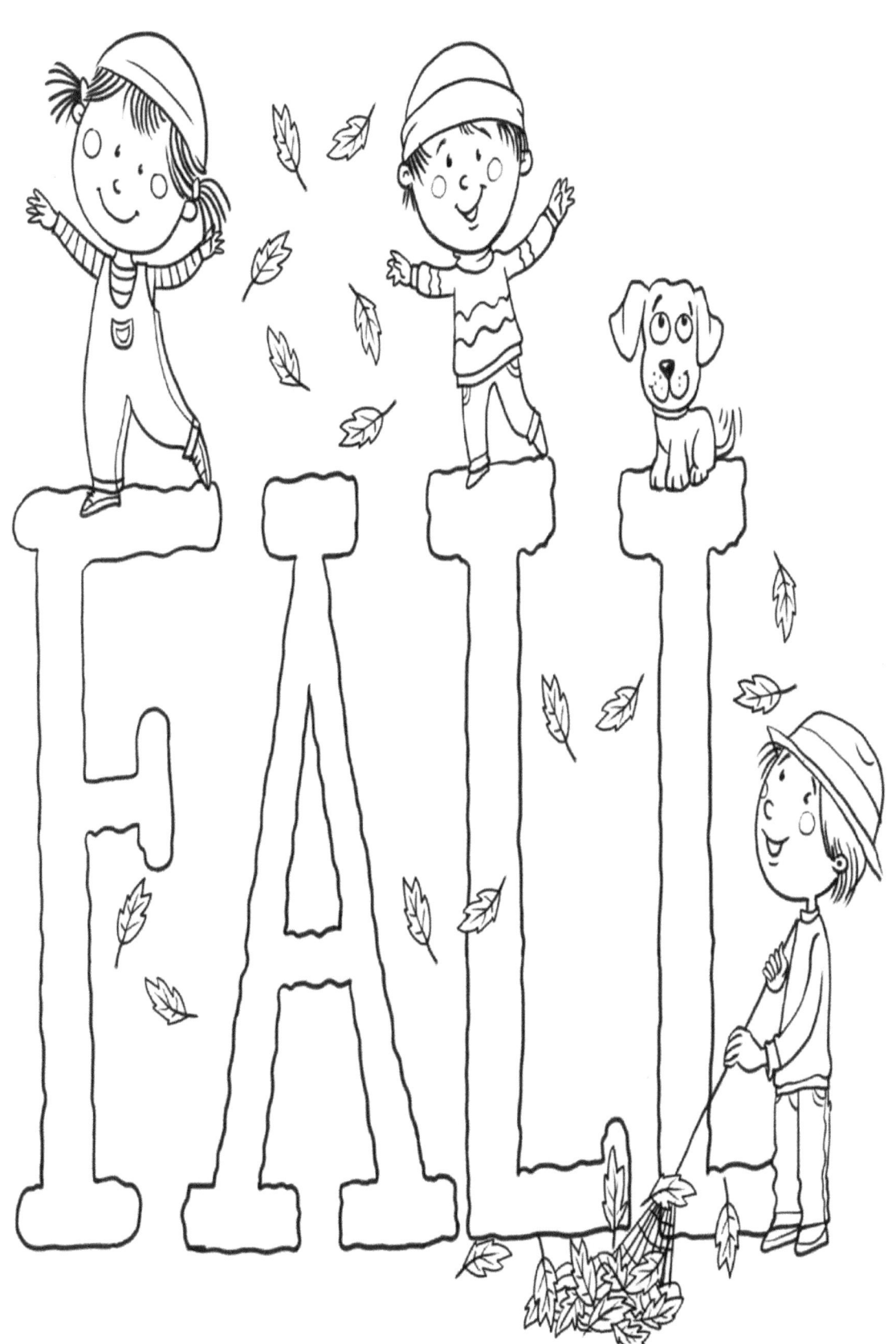

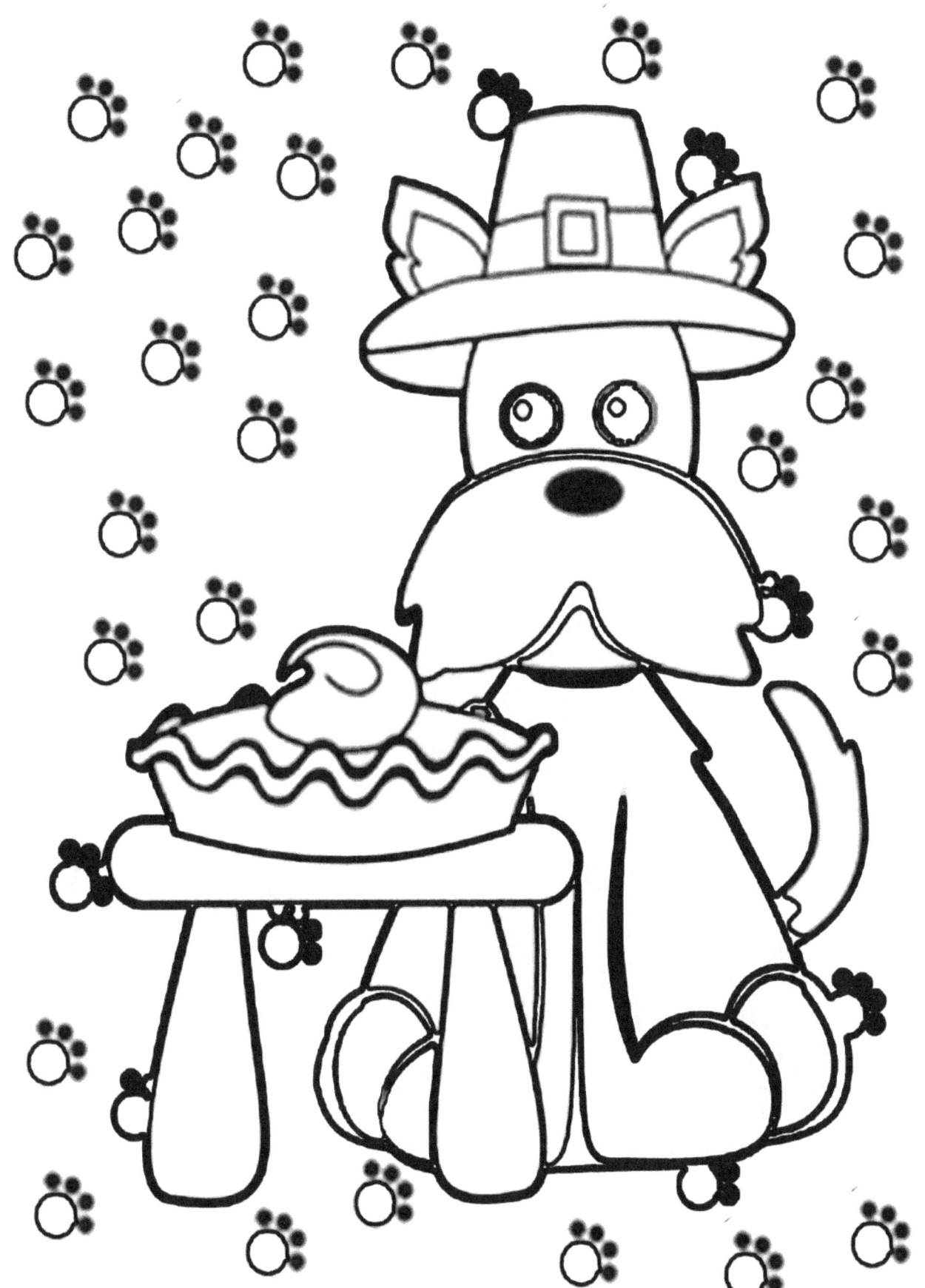

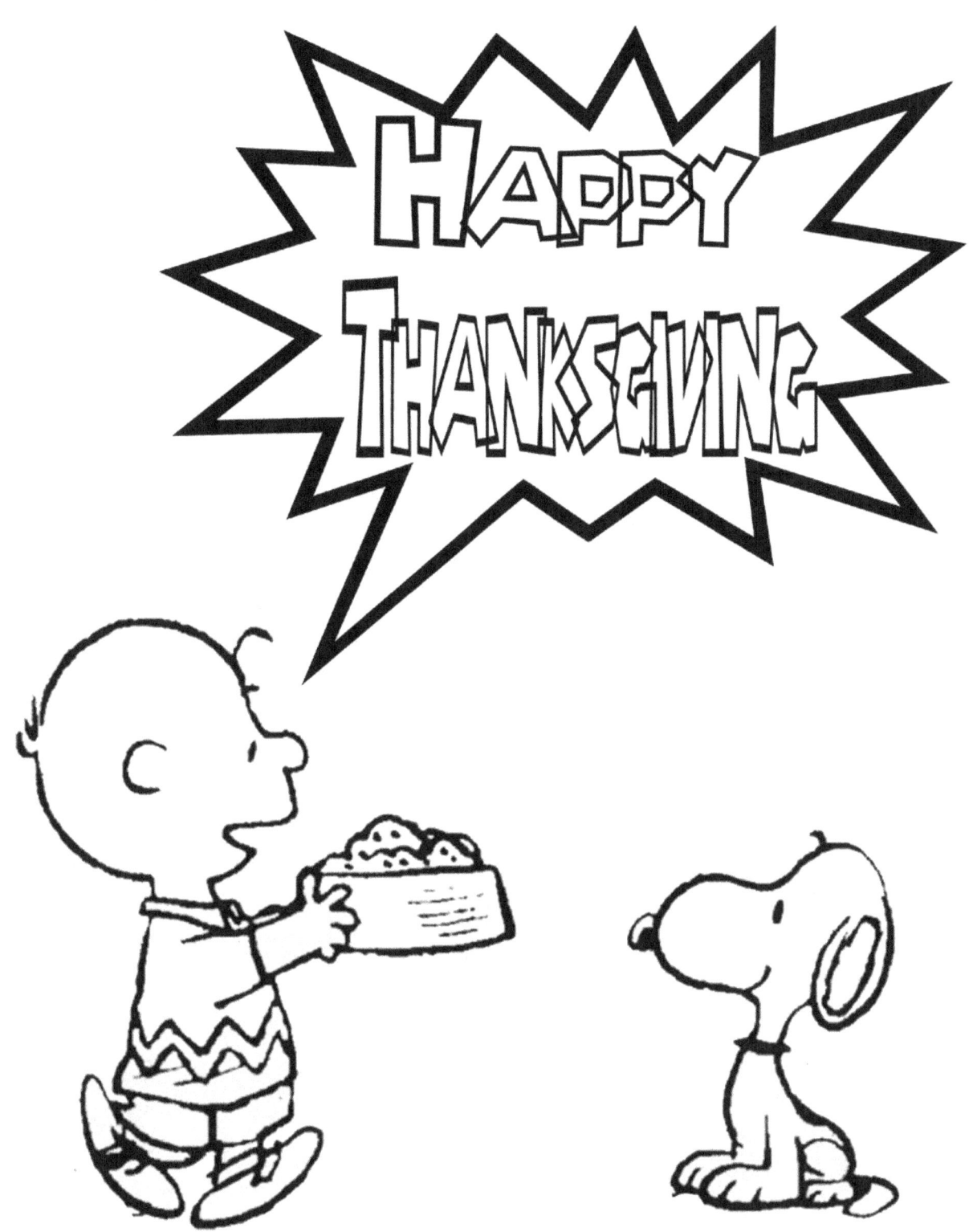

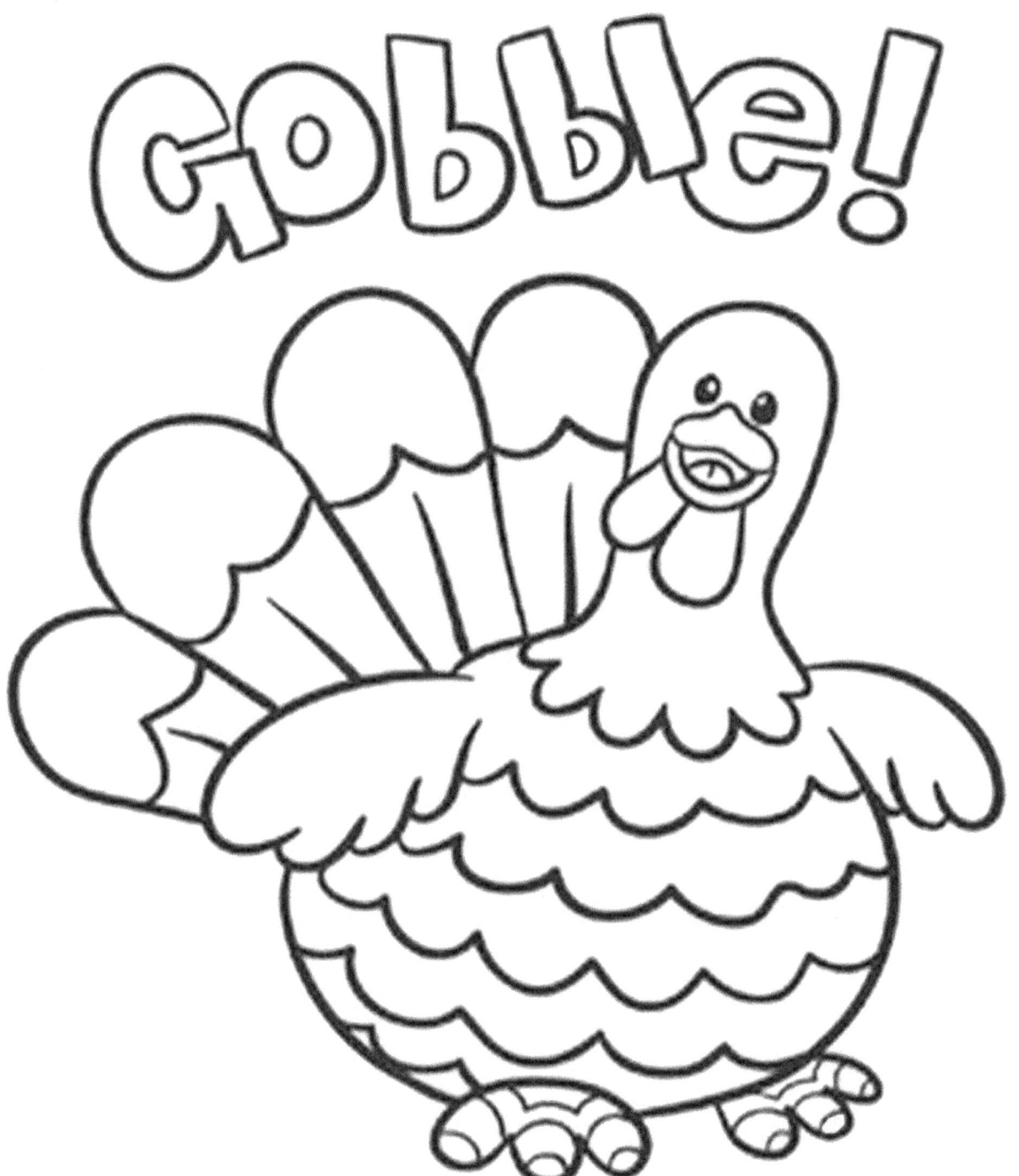

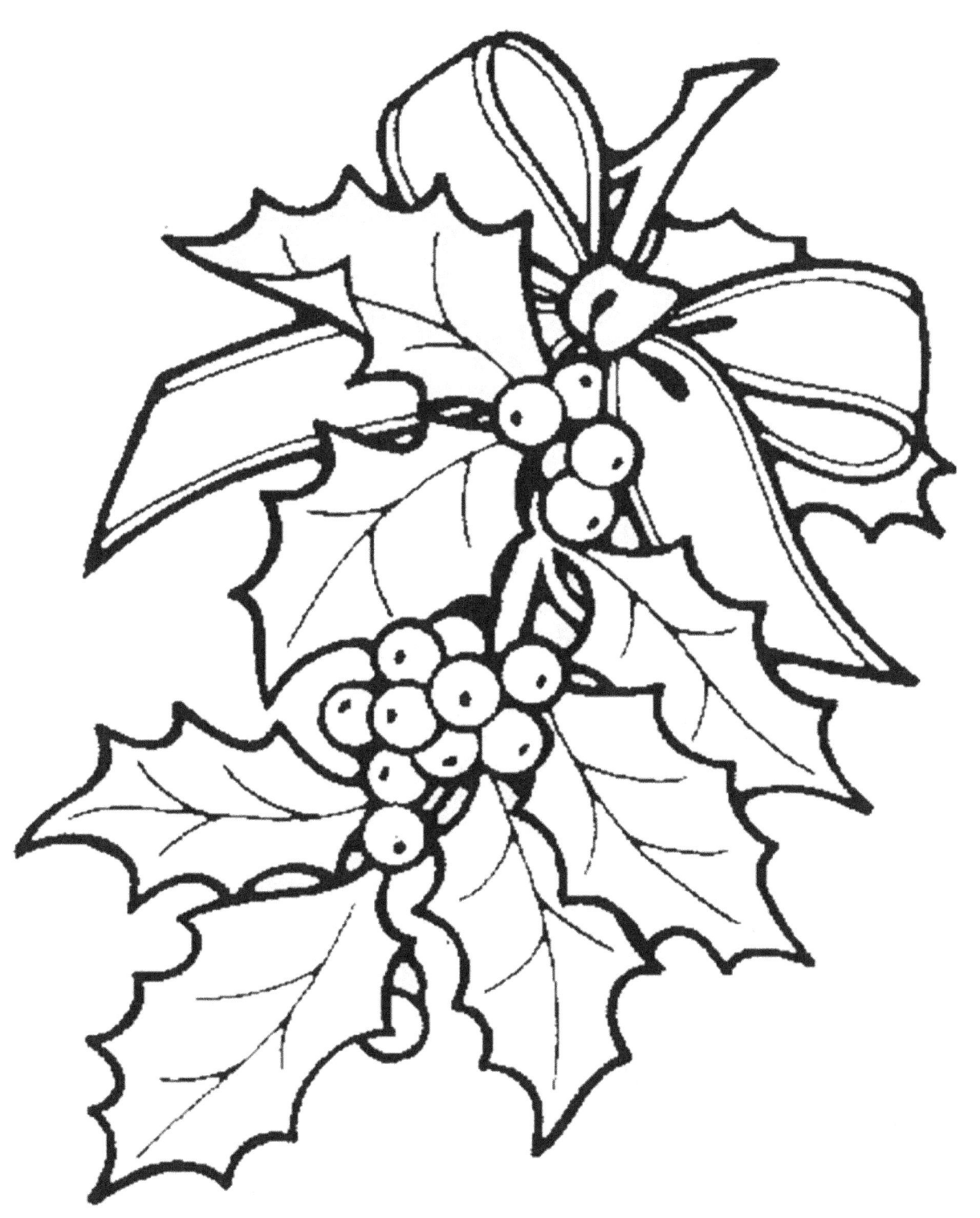

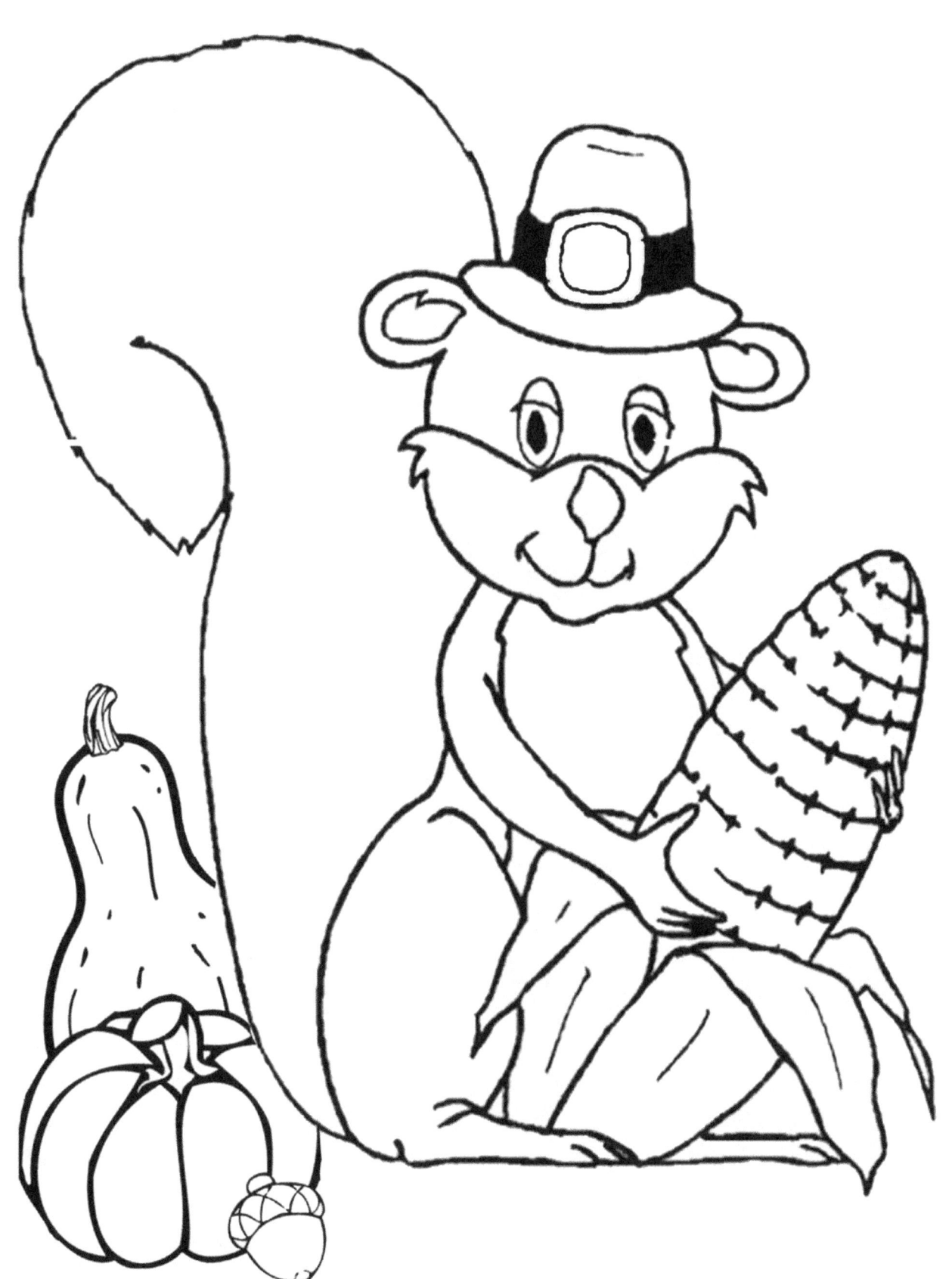

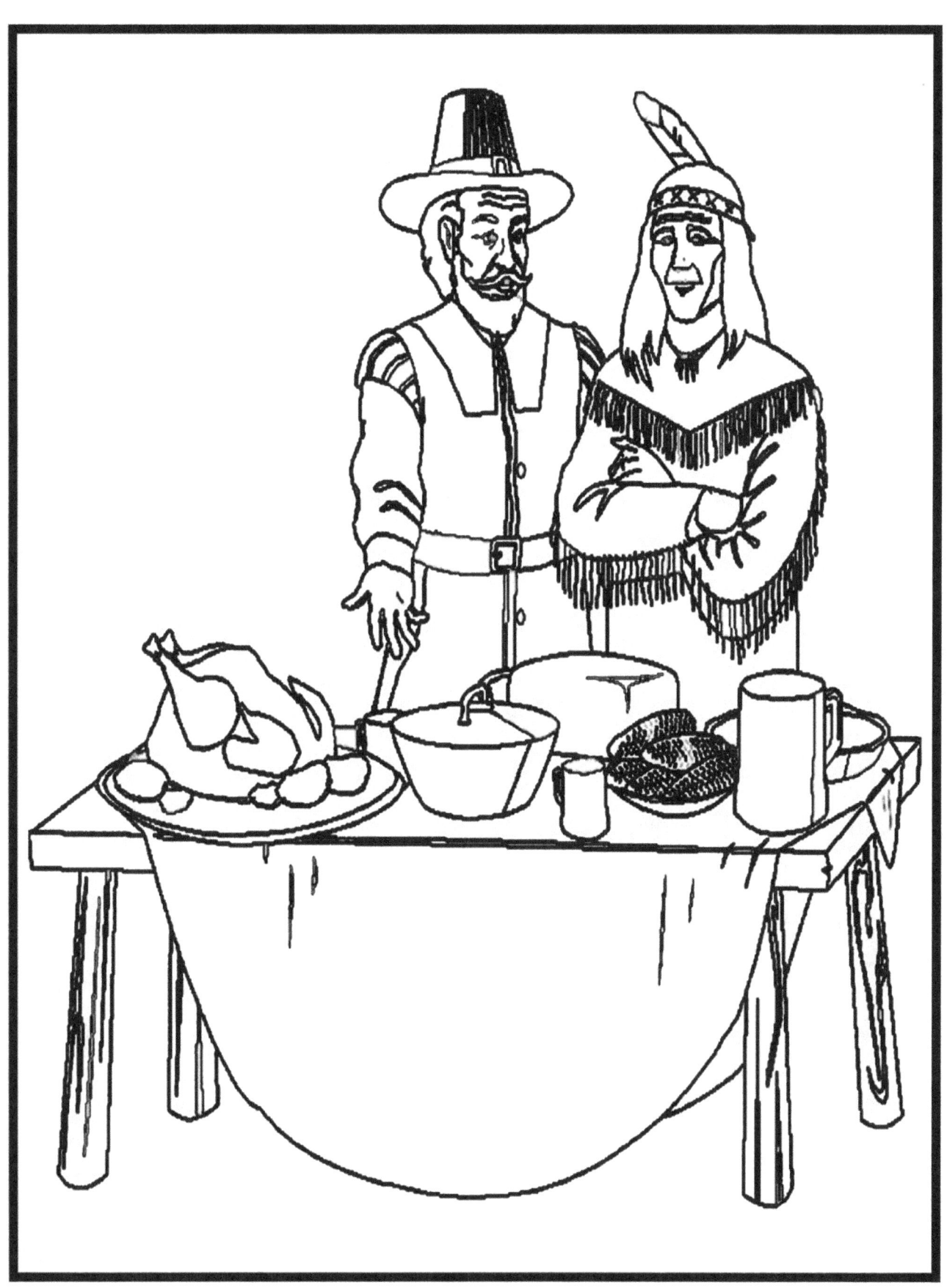

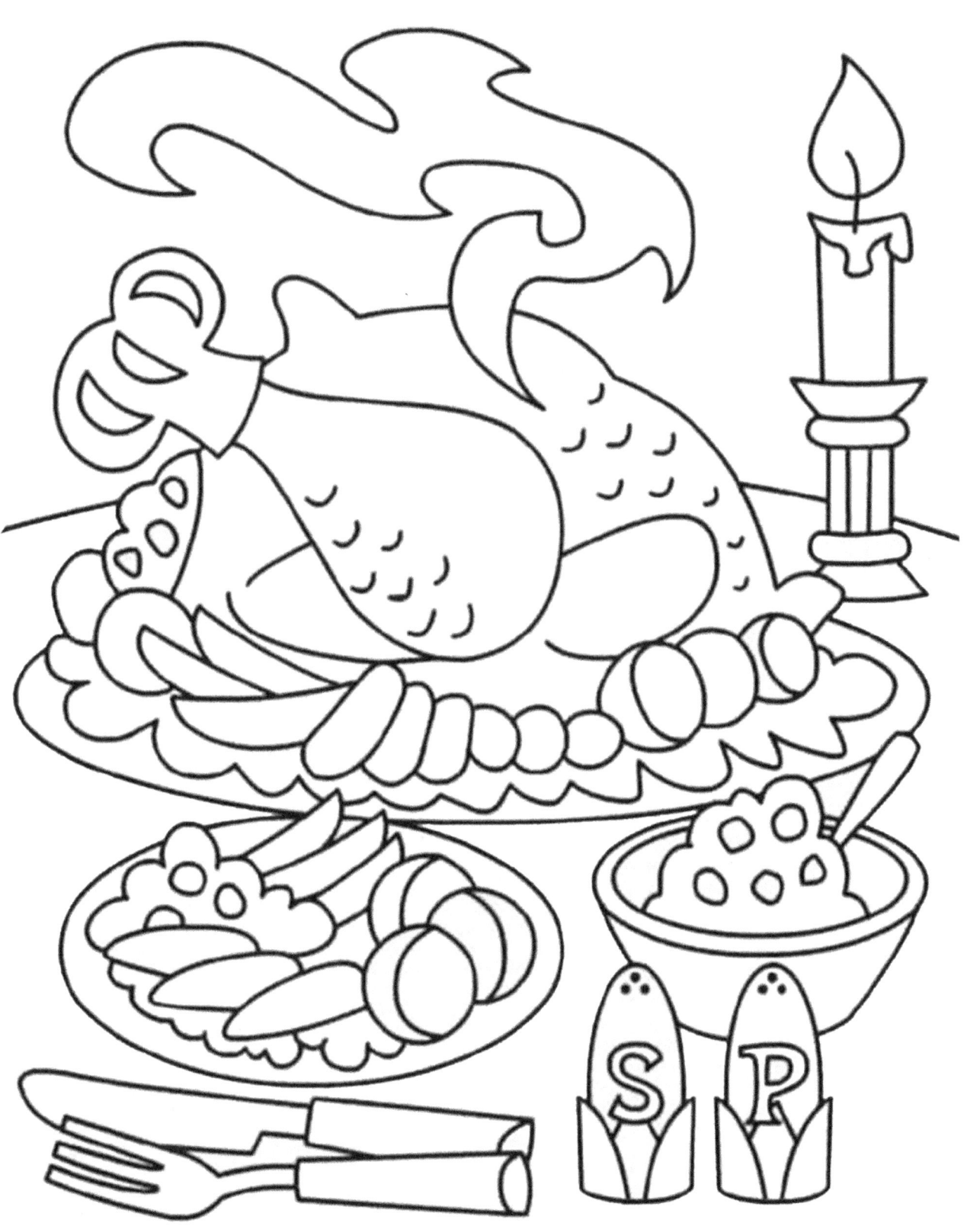

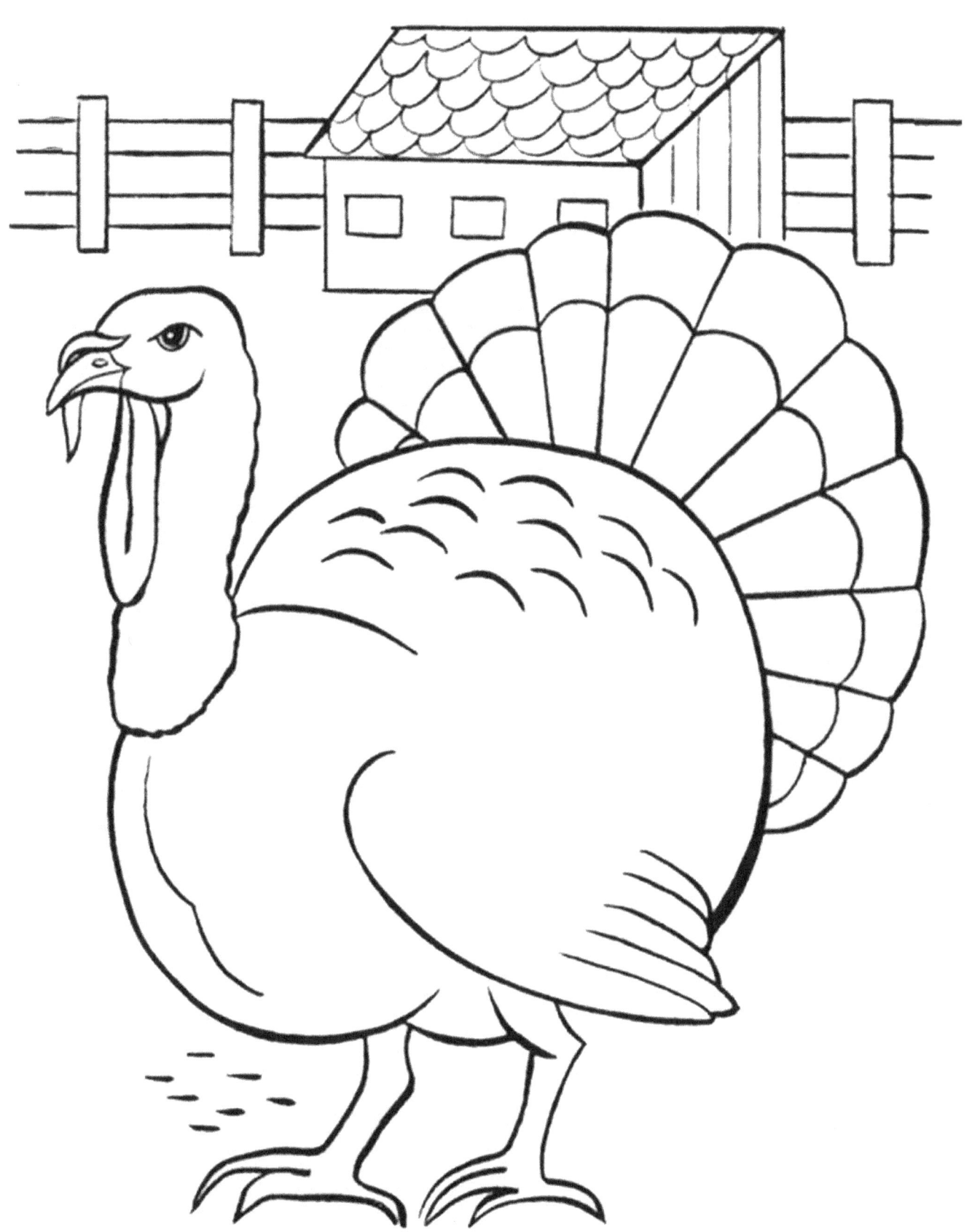

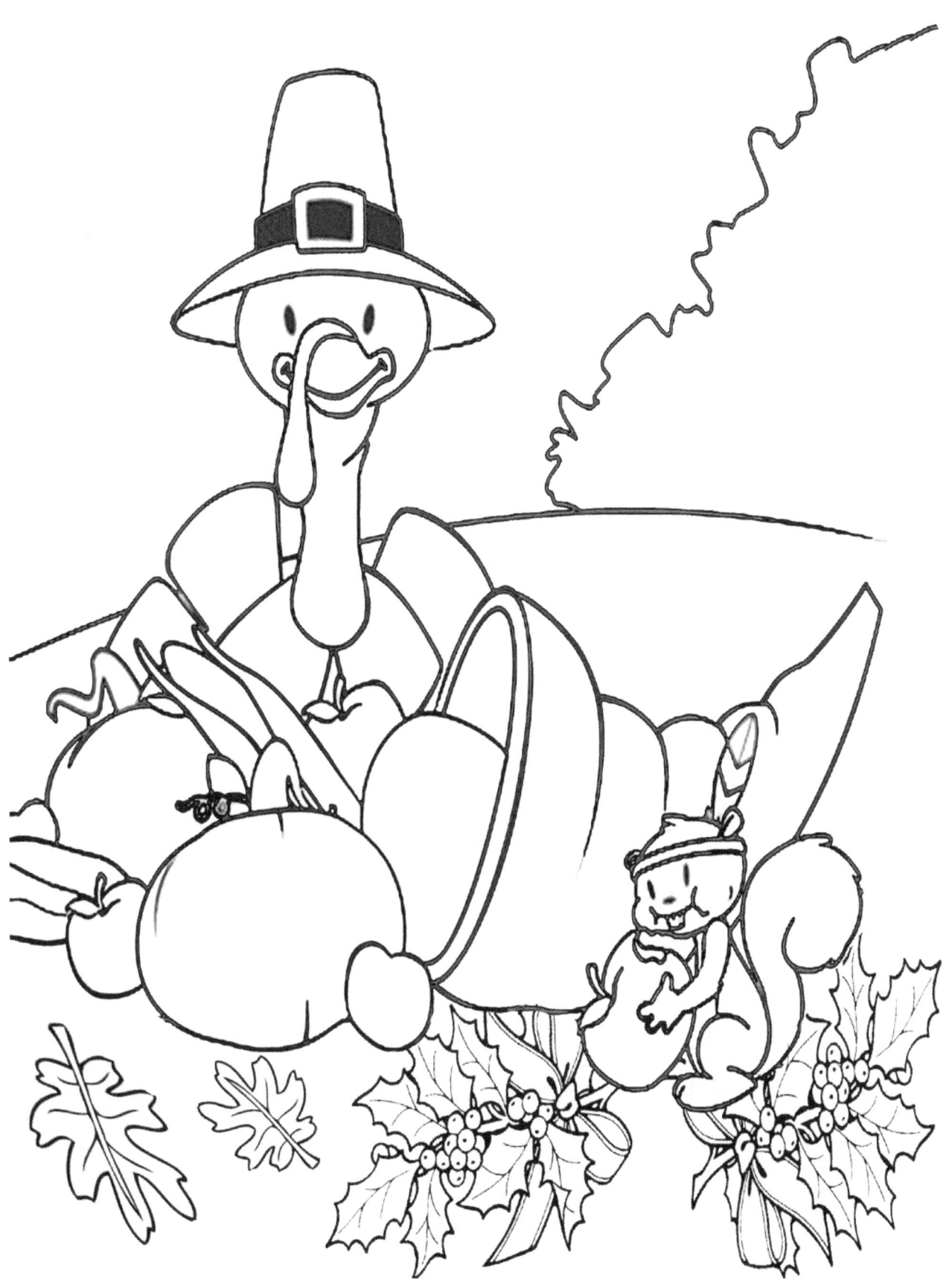

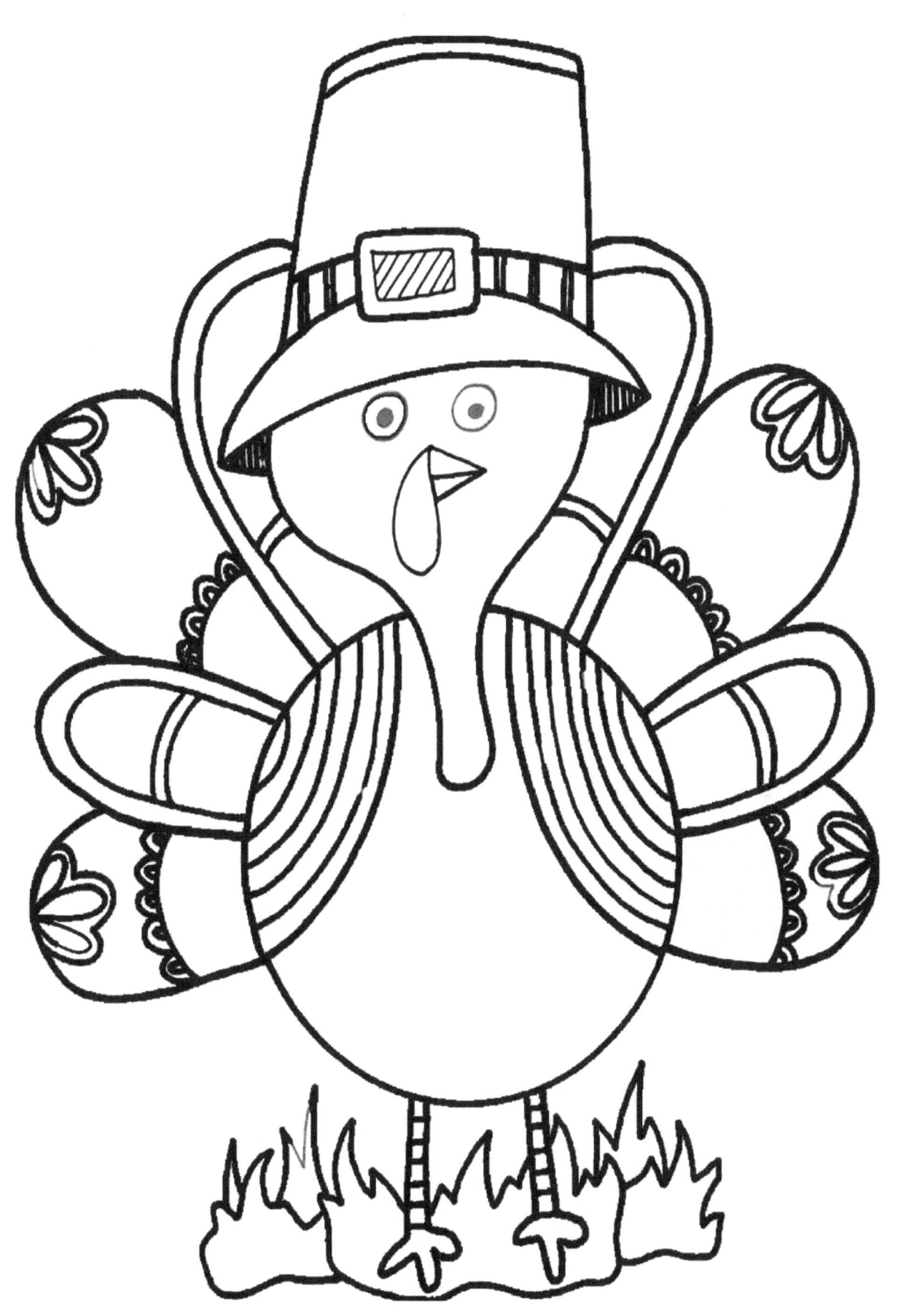

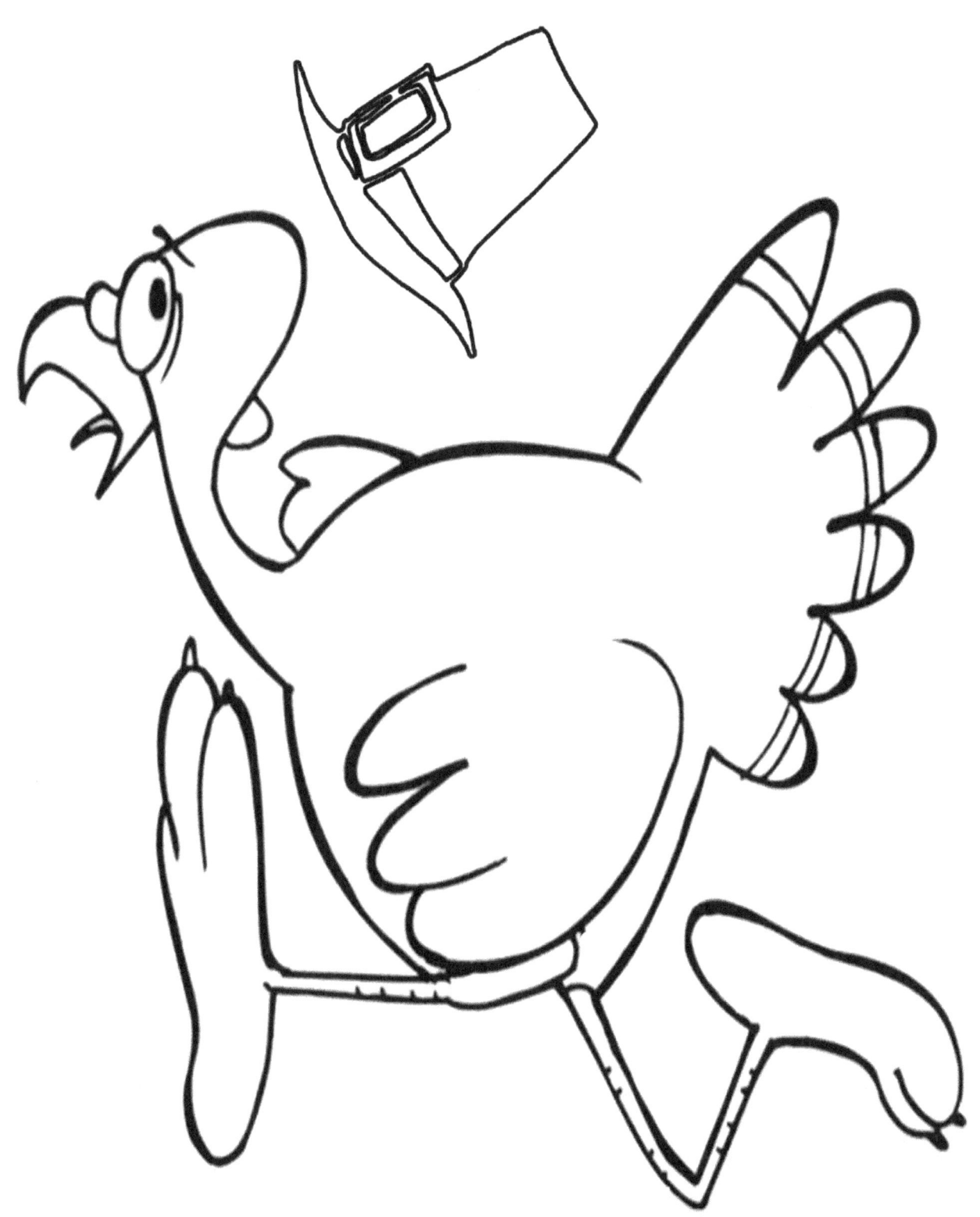

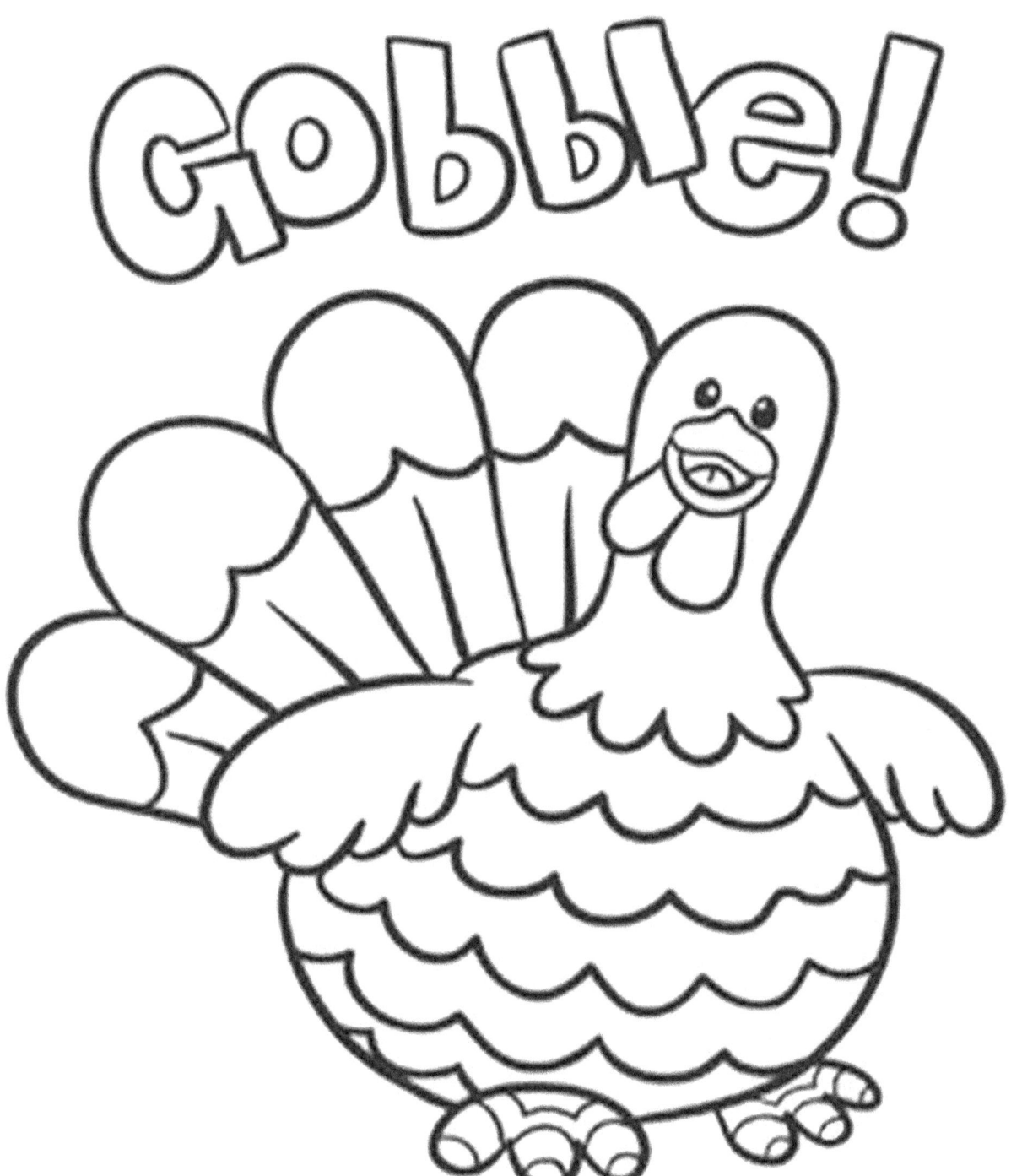

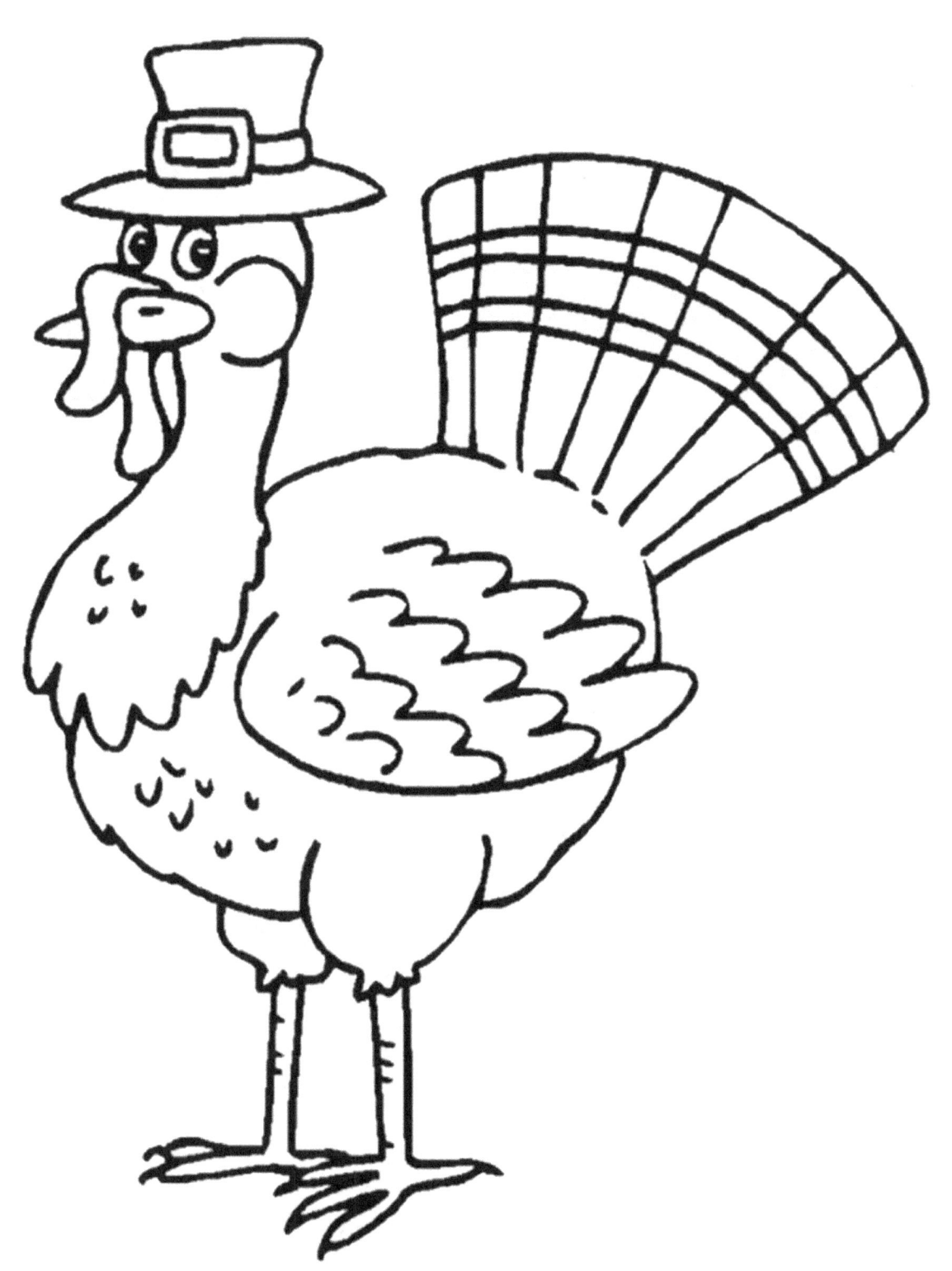

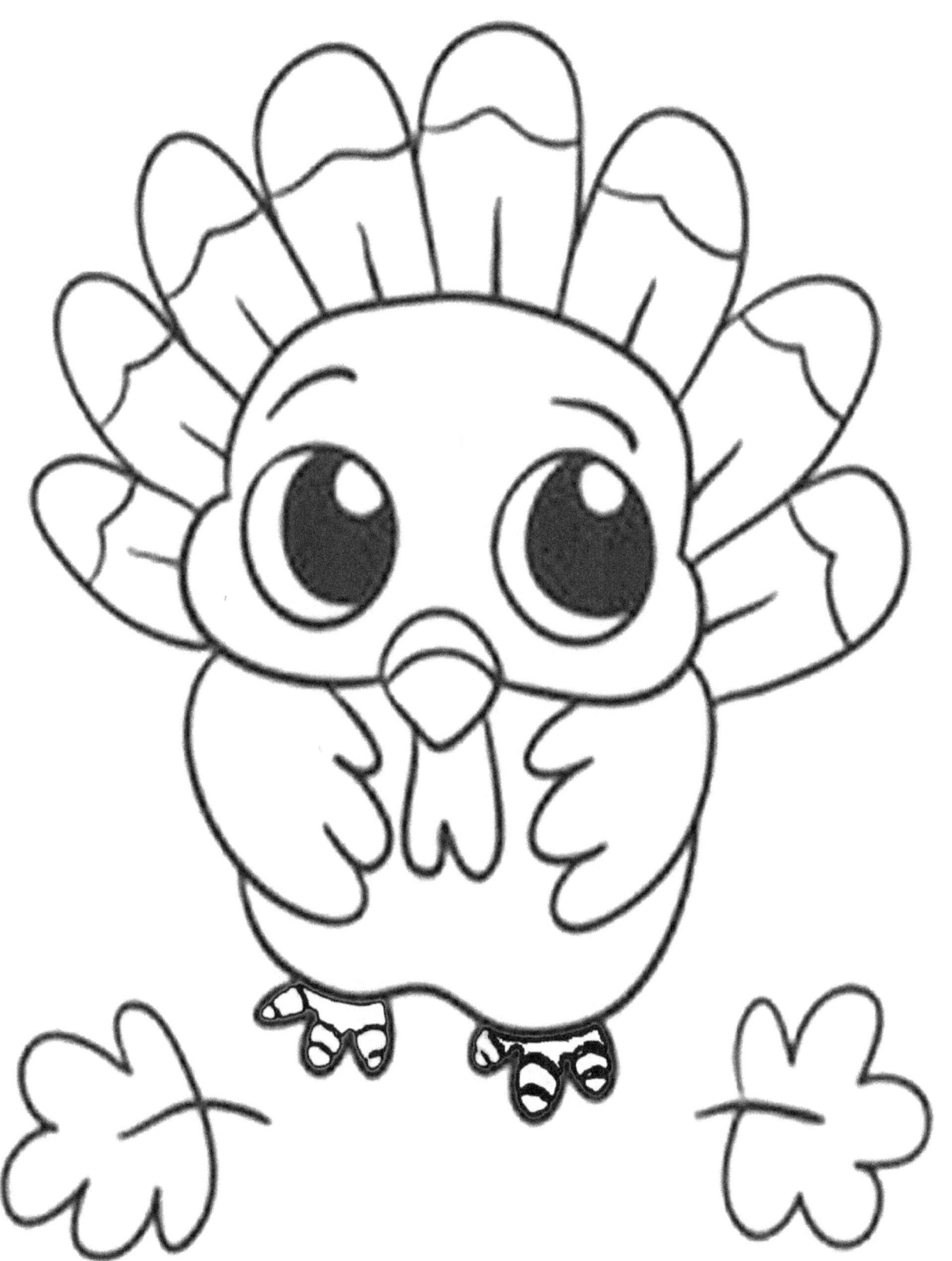

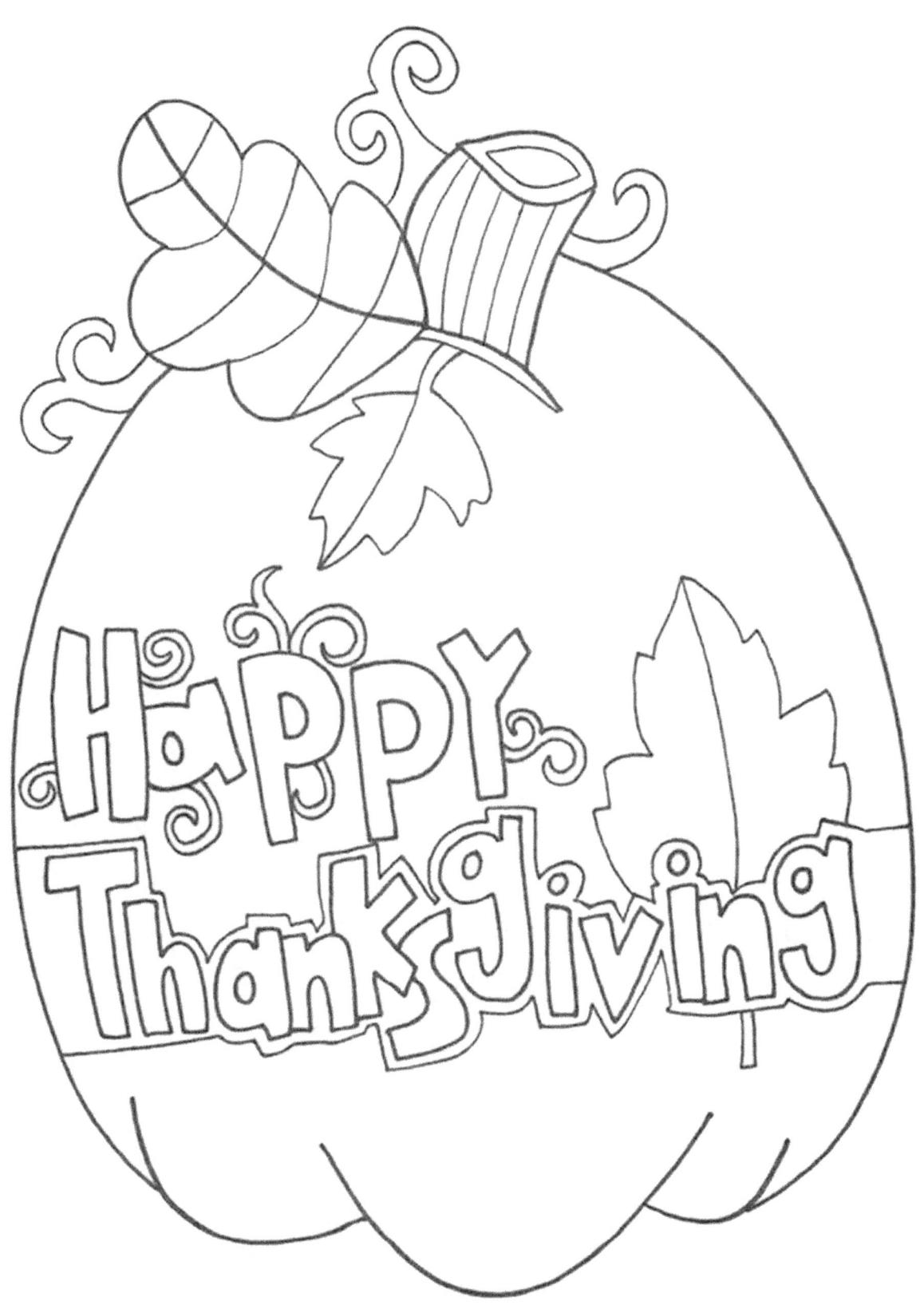

www.ingramcontent.com/pod-product-compliance
Lightning Source LLC
Chambersburg PA
CBHW082339220526
45470CB00008B/2572